**POI**

C000283183

# IT'S LIKE YOU

# MEANT

# SOMETHING

JAYMES B. LAZARO

And if you ever find
yourself in my words.
I'm sorry.

As I lay here all alone I try to imagine
the worst part of it all. I try my best to not think
about you but the timing is never wrong.
How do you love other men?
I'm curious to know, darling I need to feel,
I need to feel something. How do you love other
men? I'm curious to know because clearly
I was the fool who fell in love with you.
It breaks my heart knowing I wasn't enough.
I've become distant and I know you've noticed.
I think you see this as a game but it's game over
because I finally accepted my faith. In times, you
told me that you loved me. I still don't know in what
way. I guess you never really loved me because
here I lay in pain and there you stand.
I think I feel broken actually, I don't know how I
feel. I'm leaving. I must. But before I go
tell me, can you really love? or was it just me?
I'm sorry I wasn't man enough to make you fall in
love with me.
How do you love other men?


-Jaymes B. Lazaro

When it comes to you,
I don't know how I feel.
You tell me you don't care
and sometimes I believe you.
You tell me that it was my fault
I am the one to blame.
I put my heart into it.
And you tell me I should've
known better, better in what way?
I ask, in knowing someone like
you could never love someone like me.
I cry in pain and you seem to smile with joy.
From the start, I was just a game to you
from my end, I truly loved you.

-Jaymes B. Lazaro

I tell you how I feel
how you make me feel.
I let you know you drive me insane.
I tell you I might be falling in love with you.
And all you have to say
is shit
bullshit.
It hurts.
All my friends tell me I should drop it
but I don't listen.
And when I cry because of you
I have no one to talk to
because I was already told I was just
your killing time partner.

-Jaymes B. Lazaro

How many drinks will you need to love me? Do I need to get you drunk for you to feel me? I crave you and you know that. The things you wear make me insane. The things you whisper to my ear take me to my grave. You know the things you do to me. You know exactly how I feel. But yet all you do is play with me. You said you've told me many times "just friends" but you continue to sip another drink. And the more you drink the, more you notice me. Am I only in your mind when you are drunk? I'm confused now. Do you want me or only when you drink? Please explain yourself. Don't you dare say "nothing" again. Because the more you say it, the more I believe it. So, what is it really? Can you only accept your feelings for me only when you are drinking? Because that is how you are making it seem. You take another drink. Do you love me now? Or are you the one drinking but I'm the one who is getting drunk? Drunk in the illusion of you loving me. Don't you think I've noticed? The more you drink, the more you want me. But the more you drink, the less I want you. So please continue changing. Next time dye your hair pink. Next time wear less clothing. Next time continue laying with more men. The more you change, the more I stop loving you. You are different now. You've changed so much because of the way he hurt you. And now this is your true self. How many drinks until you can love me? Actually, keep drinking because the more you drink, the less I love you. And that is what I need. I need stop trying to find something good in you because there is nothing good to be found.

-Jaymes B. Lazaro

The feeling has changed. I was only under your
spell for a couple of months and I can officially say
I'm over it. If you want to continue being a monster
at love then I'll leave you to it. I can't be a part of
someone who has no heart. I tried. Don't you dare
not believe that. But the moment I tasted your lips.
I didn't feel it. No butterflies. Nothing. I felt nothing.
And that's when I knew. I was under the illusion
that I loved you but I never actually did. Confusing,
right? That's what your lips did to my heart
I'm done, this time I promise.

-Jaymes B. Lazaro

*Alps Drive*

I simply asked if I could kiss you
expecting a rejection you replied with
"why do you ask?"
in which I took it as a form of
"stop asking and do it"
which I did.
I leaned close to you
but your lips beat me to it.
The next thing I remember,
was you biting my lip.
I kept trying to give you a slow kiss,
but you continued to rush through it.
It wasn't what I envisioned.
I'm not disappointed I just wasn't satisfied.
May I have another chance to change the way we
kissed? Let the softness of my lips take control of
you, allow me to make you feel infinite.

-Jaymes B. Lazaro

As tears fall from my eyes
my heart starts to beat again.
I wipe away my tears
but I am afraid of what I am feeling.
I can't hide it anymore.
I might be in love.
God, I'm scared.
I don't want to hurt again
the first girl broke me in ways
that can't be fixed.
But she's not her.
I want to try things, but I'm scared
I won't be able to love as strong as I did.
I don't know if I can give love a second
chance but then I see her, and I know.
Fuck,
I'm in love with her.

-Jaymes B. Lazaro

From the moment that I met you
I never thought you would mean so much.
When I see you all I want to do is hold you
protect you and make you happy.
You are beautiful
and I don't know in what way to tell you.
I've been falling in love with you,
and I am scared
you call me "dude" and "friend"
and that makes a clear message.
I'm in love with you.
From your eyes, I'm just a friend
who you will never fall in love with.

-Jaymes B. Lazaro

I seek other women
to try and understand if what I want
from you is more than lust.
When I'm with them
I imagine that they are you.
I kiss them wishing it was your lips
I fuck them wishing it was
you scratching my
back moaning in my ear
screaming for more.
You're my biggest wonder.
I yearn to get lost in your body.
Now I understand,
it's not lust that I covet
it's your soul that I want
to ravage in these sheets.

-Jaymes B. Lazaro

Blue,
that's what I feel when I see you.
Your beauty is as beautiful
as the morning sky,
your heart is as dark
blue as the deep sea.
You're like a canvas.
The color blue is your
only expression.
Stop being afraid of showing
your multi-colors.
Allow an artist in your life
allow him to revive the
art that you are.

-Jaymes B. Lazaro

I get jealous when you talk to other
men I know, it's wrong of me
I shouldn't be this way.
You have the right to please
yourself with him
I get jealous, and I'll admit it.
I hate knowing
you are allowing him to get closer
to you, more than you've let me.
I guess it's not jealousy that I fear
it's the thought that I will never
have you that kills me.

-Jaymes B. Lazaro

I opened up to you in ways
that I've never done before.
I gave you my heart
through my writing
through my words
through my actions.
You continue to say
that you are not what I want
that I deserve better.
I don't know what is better than you,
but I am eager to find out.
I'm done chasing you.
I'm done trying to prove that
you are right for me.
If you can't see it,
then stay blind
I finally opened my eyes
from the illusion of you.

-Jaymes B. Lazaro

Life is hard
especially, when you are in love.
Why is love so hard to keep up with?
There is not much that I can say to
prove that love is hard.
Only the thought of an almost
lover that returns to mind.
Love is not the hard part
the way she loved was.
She wasn't a hopeless
romantic like I am,
and that's what made it hard.
I desired a forever
while she just wanted
a brief moment.

-Jaymes B. Lazaro

My mouth hasn't shut up
since you kissed it.
Please do it again
do that biting thing that you do.
Let our next kiss lead us
into making love for the first time.

-Jaymes B. Lazaro

## Making love

Do you think we can lose control just for
one night? I need to feel your body close.
I need to please you just this one time let
me get over this craving of you one night
that's all I ask. I'll do things to you that will
leave the softness of my lips imprinted all over
your body. First, I'll kiss you passionately and
whisper in your ear, how beautiful you are.
As we kiss, I'll run my hands through your body
memorizing the softness of your skin. While
mastering your body, I'll remove your shirt and
your bra leaving you half naked. I'll move my
kisses from your lips down to your neck and I'll
start to feel your heartbeat rising, and your skin turn
to lava. I'll put my hands on your breast taking my
time admiring their perfect symmetry. I'll start to
kiss your breast leading my way on to sucking them
as you moan and pull my hair. I'll guide myself
down to your waist. I'll remove your pants and
leave you with just your panties. There, I'll have
you exactly how I want you. I'll take myself back to
your lips and push you against the wall. I'll rush my
fingers down to your panties, and I'll finger fuck
you. You'll be screaming and moaning trying to
catch your breath but I won't allow you. I'll go
down on my knees and start to kiss your bottom
lips. Fuck, you'll be so wet I'll be able to feel your
juices dripping on my tongue. You'll orgasm, and
I'll finally allow you to catch your breath. I'll stand
up, and I'll see your face reeking in sweat you'll
push me closer to your naked body, and you'll

whisper in my ear you want me inside you. I'll tease you and tell you "not yet" I'll pick you up from your thighs and escort you to our bedroom I'll lay you down in our bed (You are even more beautiful naked) I'll stare at you for one long second respecting your naked soul, you'll be moaning my name, begging me to be inside you. I'll spread your legs wide open and guide myself deep in you as I'm stroking in and out of you making good love. I'll guide the way I please you by the noises you make. Baby, I don't know how long I can last with you moaning crazy begging me not to stop. We will both orgasm at the same time, and I'll feel your body shivering you'll grab me by my sweaty hair and rest my head between your hands you'll look me straight in the eyes and tell me "I love you" I'll kiss you and tell you "I love you too" what a beautiful night. Making love to the love of my life if only you would lose control with me tonight. If only.

-Jaymes B. Lazaro

You're hard
you're cold
you don't let yourself to
be loved anymore.
You have given up
you no longer believe
in beautiful love.
You hide behind many walls
so, people won't see you hurt.
You act like you are a solid rock
you act like you are nothing at all.
If only you knew you are a diamond
in the human eye.

-Jaymes B. Lazaro

*La Feria*

Last night I couldn't stop staring at you. You looked
amazing. The bright lights complimented your skin,
the way your colored hair shined made my heart
stop, that smile you made after you were fed was
fucking cute as hell. So many women and you were
the only one I kept my eyes on. Do you have any
idea how bad I wanted you? I wanted to hold you,
kiss you and tell you that I love you. I did ask you
to get lost with me just for a second and you
rejected me. Once again, and again as much as I
wanted you, I could not make you want me. I had to
control myself and that's the reason why at times I
was a dick. I was afraid. I was so close to telling
you "I love you" but, I didn't want to be a fool who
said it out loud and be rejected. So, I said nothing.
Now I will wait for the day I know for sure you feel
the same way maybe that will be in two years or
maybe that will never be. Until then I'll see you
with other men and I'll continue to lay with other
women. Until then I hope you realize that I'm the
man who deserves to oneday call you my wife.

-Jaymes B. Lazaro

I explain the way I see
life to so many people
but none of them have
viewed life the same as I do.
Which makes me afraid
when will I find the one who
sees the way I see?

-Jaymes B. Lazaro

*The story of I made up, right?*

It all changed once your hair changed color. It was like a switch. I realized I had feelings for you, but I still wasn't quite sure in what way. I told you many times that I might love you. And your response was always "it's not love-it's an obsession" and that the moment our bodies met with sweat and pleasure, I would get "over it". We continued to talk, and I started to know you- the parts that you allowed me to know, you are very secure you didn't like to get close, and you didn't want to fall in love. While I got the chance to know you, I realized that I cared for you and that I needed you. Feeling that way made me afraid because I knew I was the only one falling and knowing that destroyed a bit of me every day. As I continued to fall you, you continued to push me away harder and harder each time. Then we had our first kiss I feel as if you rushed through it because you wanted to get it over with. Feeling your lips on my lips just confirmed how much I craved you. After that kiss, you would make comments such as "it never happened" and "don't tell anyone" I always asked you if it was because you were embarrassed but you would always deny it. And then I left work. The chances of seeing you went from every other day to maybe once a week. The times I saw you I made sure to taste your lips. Since we didn't see each other as much, we would text all day and talk on the phone for hours. You made me laugh like no other. When I thought, you were letting me in you would then clarify and say we were "just friends" I'm sorry, but I don't go around kissing people who are just my "friend" you made it seem like that was normal. Then our "friendship" went from talking to fighting. I am not a jealous person, but the thought of losing you to someone else made me lose my shit. I will admit that my stupidity was one of the main reason we started to fade away. The weird thing is the more we fought, the more I sexually craved you, and I may sound like a complete asshole, but I desired you so much that I once believed that was the reason I stayed. Then that one Sunday night happened at you know whose house. I know you were craving it as much as I was. I enjoyed every minute of it. And then it happened again outside your house in my car. Fuck, I needed to make love to you, but I also wanted your heart, you made it clear that I will never have both. We both picked different things, I picked your heart but you didn't pick mine. Then that one moment happened remember? When we were kissing in my car outside your house you stopped kissing me, and you rested my head between your hands, and there you said it "te quiero" I smiled and I said it back. That's the memory I still to this day hold on to. But with us, there were not so many good memories. We fought again and like I've said before we both said stupid shit and that's when you made it clear that you didn't want anything to do with me you started to say how "there was never an us, I never loved you, I never saw myself with you" at that moment, I understood the woman you wanted me to know. I knew I had to leave. So, I walked away. Not because you destroyed me, not because I stopped loving you but because I realized we will never have a happy relationship. We may both enjoy each other's company, but we are toxic to each other. I'm sorry I am a dick, and I'm sorry this never worked out. I still think of you. I'm sorry I couldn't make your heart beat again. I don't regret our first kiss, and I hope you don't regret it either. In my own twisted way, I will always care for you. Don't forget me. Because I will never forget you. I love you. Maybe in a couple of years, we might be right for each other. Maybe.

-Jaymes B. Lazaro

*With time*

I will admit, I am afraid to love. Not only to
love but to love you. The way you carry yourself
scares me. Because many have failed to understand
you, and I am afraid I'll fail miserably like the
others. I just love how you push me away. Thinking
maybe I'll give up and move on. But you couldn't
be more wrong. All it took was one kiss, I was
totally hooked. Addicted to you. The harder you
push me away, the more reasons you give me to
stay. I've made mistakes, Perhaps I pressure you too
much. But if I've proven anything by the constant
nagging to win your heart, I've proven that you do
have a heart, a heart you claim you no longer have.
You're patient with me. You know how I am and
what I need to make me happy. And I know what
makes me happy is hard for you to say, but in given
times and given moments. You show me that one
emotion you are so afraid of. But I know, trust me- I
know. I don't want to pressure you, I just want you
to let me love you, all of you. You've changed, and
I know you've noticed. This new person that you've
become I joke around and take full credit of. The
truth is, that's all you. I'm just lucky enough to be
in your life and watch you grow. Allow me to stay,
open up to me. Show me more of who you are.
Allow me to continue feeding this fire that we both
know keeps us warm. Allow me to continue to solve
the mystery of your heart.

-Jaymes B. Lazaro

One day I'll eventually
stop thinking about you.
One day I'll stop to wonder if
you're kissing other lips.
One day I'll stop missing you.
I do hope one day I stop loving you
but today, today is not that day.
For now, I'll pray for a better tomorrow.

-Jaymes B. Lazaro

*Silence hurt me more than the actual truth*

My voice cracked when
I was a dick to her.
When I was telling her
how she made me feel.
My heart hurt every time I said
everything and she said nothing.

-Jaymes B. Lazaro

Next time you're getting pleased
I hope you scream my name.
Remember the way I made you feel.
When another man is inside you, remember me.
Relive the way I took control of your body
remember you would moan telling me not to stop.
Next time you're getting pleased scream my name
and understand that it was me.
It was always me.

-Jaymes B. Lazaro

You asked me to stay
but with "no feelings"
The truth is I left because
it was too late for that
I was unconditionally in love
with you since our first kiss.

-Jaymes B. Lazaro

If I ever see her with another
man that would destroy me.
So please God.
Never let me see her with him.


-Jaymes B. Lazaro

Loving you was the biggest
adrenaline I've ever lived
and it was fucking amazing.

-Jaymes B. Lazaro

I'm one step closer
from forgetting you
but I'm five steps
behind from unloving you.

-Jaymes B. Lazaro

Those eyes of yours are my weakness
your lips are my addiction
and your touch is a curse.
Yet here I am knowing you're bad for me
but you are still everything I desire.
Fuck me up.
It's ok.
Fuck me like you have never
fucked anyone before.
Destroy me.
And then tell me it was all my fault.
Fuck me over, again.
Toxic my life one more time.
Screw me over
one last time,
but please make it count.


-Jaymes B. Lazaro

I should've walked away the moment
I was crying in her face, and all she said was
"stop it you look fake" that my feelings made her
feel sick. Because she doesn't care about the hearts
she breaks and there I was, addicted to her touch.
It hurt knowing how quickly she moved on.
I never listened to the voices around me.
Where they would warn me to stop loving her.
I got in too deep, now look at me I'm the only one
who cries himself to sleep.

-Jaymes B. Lazaro

I don't want to talk about love
I just want your skin
I want your kisses
I want your juices
I want to hear you moan
I want to fuck you one last time
before I eventually leave for good.

-Jaymes B. Lazaro

Call me when you're lonely.
Let me know you still think of me.
Tell me you crave me inside you.

-Jaymes B. Lazaro

At 12:55 am that is the time where
you are on my mind the most.
Every midnight of my life
belongs to the memory of you.

-Jaymes B. Lazaro

You texted saying you missed me and if
we could give "us" another chance.
As much as I want to hold you in my arms again.
I said no.
I know how this story ends.
I'm sorry,
believe me.
I'm still in love with you.
It's time for me to let you understand
that you've lost me completely this time.
It's too late
you need to let this fade.
I don't want any trouble
I don't want any regrets
I don't want any miss understanding.
I need you to know that; I still love you
but I refuse to hurt because of you.
Not anymore
not again
never.
Make it easy and walk away,
prove you don't care.
Show me and drop me just like you
said you were going to do.


-Jaymes B. Lazaro

I thought she loved me.
I mean she would say it while she kissed me
the words of "te quiero" would
come out of her lips like poetry.
As beautiful as it sounded she would
always leave me in doubt.
When I ask for her assurance, she would
always say "I'm not going to say it again"
when I said it too much, she would say,
"you need to stop telling me you love me"
and yet I still held on.
I was still trying.
I was still hoping.
I was still left in doubt.
When everything was falling apart
I asked if we were done
all she said was
"we never had anything Jaymes"
and that's when I knew.
This whole time it was a one-sided effort
all this time I was the only one trying
all this time I was the only one who meant every
"te quiero"


-Jaymes B. Lazaro

I asked you to help me let you go.
I asked you to treat me like shit,
to ignore me. To do whatever it
takes to help me get over you.
Your response was clear
you've been doing this all along.
You ignore me
treat me like shit
and yet I'm the fool who fell
in love with that perfect woman,
I made up in my head.
She was never there
I was blinded.

-Jaymes B. Lazaro

I keep thinking with time you'll make yourself fall back into my arms. I keep telling myself we are both not ready maybe in a year, we can try it again. I keep fooling myself, deep down I know we are no good. I know the kind of love I want is not the kind you seek. I know you want a family and I can't provide that. As much as I want to leave this open to the possibility of making you mine I know that's not what you want. I am not what you want.
I tried to change my ways to please you but you never once told me you noticed. I gave and gave and all you did was take and take. I keep holding on to the memories, the good ones, of you and I and that's my problem. I miss you deeply. I want to spread your legs and feel your warmth. I want to grab your ass and hear you say it's all mine. I want you back. I want you to tell me you love me and then realize in the moment what you said. I want you to pull my hair because you know I love that shit. I want you to kiss me again and again but this will be the last time I will want you. For this last time, I will write about you until we meet again. If we meet again.

-Jaymes B. Lazaro

I want to fall in love with someone
I seek the cheesy shit.
I crave the late-night fucks
I desire the "I love you"
I want to love all of her
I want to in the end
for her to take my last name.

-Jaymes B. Lazaro

I am a good person, not perfect but good.
For a long time, I fought for her love. I tried everything. I changed my ways to try and make her fall in love with me, while I was falling for her, she was falling in love with herself. She was growing. The more she grew the more my heart fell for her. I could see in her eyes she was opening up to me but her words made sure I didn't feel too confident she was mine. In the end, I told her I hated her. For a second I did. Later, I regretted every word I said. As the weeks passed by I started to understand her reasons. She wasn't scared to love me. She was afraid of the future she would have with me. I was worse than her ex she once told me she was done with that type of "love" I fought for her. My love for her was stronger than my pride but I stopped trying- I gave up. I didn't send that draft message because I knew she was tired. She told me she didn't want me in her life and I asked if she stopped loving me she said, "did I say that?" I am a quitter. I quit her love. She still owns my heart but we are best staying apart.

-Jaymes B. Lazaro

We are two broken people who need love again.
Real love from someone who gives us real love.
I'm not going to argue this, but anyone can love
you.
Look at you.
You're everything. But what am I?
What am I to you?
Am I just another man you play with?
Am I another man you use to forget him for one
night
and the moment he contacts you again
will you fall back into his arms?
So, tell me.
Who am I to you?
Was I nothing?
Was I just another joke?
Was I another night?
I will always wonder who I was in your eyes
if I ever hold a place in your heart
if I ever made you feel infinite.

-Jaymes B. Lazaro

When you texted saying you were tired of
repeating yourself to me on how we were nothing
and how you don't love me, and you never did.
That night, those words, those feeling- destroyed
me. I had trouble sleeping, and I decided I wasn't
going to sleep alone. That night I used a naked body
to try and forget you. I fucked the shit out of her.
I fucked her angry. Knowing how she felt about me
I wanted to fuck up her life the same way you had
fucked up mine. Fucking her gave her hope,
as she moaned, she whispered in my ear "I love
you" I looked her straight in the eyes, and I said it
back knowing I didn't feel it knowing I would never
give her my last name the words of "I love you"
came out of my mouth. In that second, I realized
how easy it was to say it how easy it was for you to
tell me "te quiero" how easy it was to lie to my face
while I was close into cumming, the memory of you
helped me finish-I almost moaned your name.
My way home was pathetic I felt sick. This game
that you master is not for me in one night, you
turned me into a monster in one night, you made me
realized who I truly was. You didn't destroy me
you gave me strength. Ironic I know. I am a good
fucking person. I will not allow a narcissist change
who I am anymore my way home was
metamorphic.

-Jaymes B. Lazaro

05.01.2018

I knew she was married
and I didn't give a fuck.
I know it was a sin,
but it felt fucking good doing it.
Our excuse was always
"We have history"
So, it's alright.
She would still tell me she loves me,
even when she married another man.
I never once said it back because
I never loved her to begin with.
The last time I saw her I came and left.
And I haven't replied to her texts ever since.
A dick move I know,
but I promised myself I'll never be
that type of man anymore.

-Jaymes B. Lazaro

*5.23.18*

While you are out there celebrating your birthday.
I sit here trying my best to not think of you.
I don't know why I still have not let you go.
I think of you every day-it drives me insane.
You made your Instagram public and
all I can see are the flowers your new lover has
gotten you.
I was angry at first
I was hurt
I even almost cried.
But hey, you did that to me too
you showed off the things I gave you
and now that I'm no longer an interest of yours
you deleted every trace of me.
You'll do the same to him or who knows
maybe you'll learn to love him.
I don't hate you.
I just don't understand.
I'm trying so hard to close this
door of you and move on.
Believe me
I'm trying.
Happy birthday.
Hopefully next year today,
I won't even remember your name.

-Jaymes B. Lazaro

*I promised you sunflowers on your birthday*

It's a beautiful Wednesday morning. Without hesitation, I bought you the sunflowers I promised. I'm driving, getting closer to your neighborhood by the minute. I'm debating whether or not to show up on your front door and sing to you happy birthday. Tears are falling. I'm so in love with you. My love for you is strong, but the words you used to destroy me are stronger. I took the next exit, and I drove home. I was going to do it, just like what I did with the frame. I was going to leave the sunflowers on your car and walk away. I even wrote you a letter. A letter I did not sign, I did not want you to know it was from me. Because I know you would probably laugh. I bought you the sunflowers I promised. But I'm keeping them. Happy birthday, hermosa. Have a good one.

-Jaymes B. Lazaro

I see you're talking to your ex
you're talking to another man.
I can't blame you
I can't hate you.
I see you're drinking almost every weekend
you're complaining of having mental breakdowns.
I watched how you drained your life with sleep.
I see all of this, and it made me realize.
I don't know you, I never did.
Then you say you are glad people can see you're
living your best life but then I see the excessive
drinking splatter all over your wall.
The only one you're fooling is yourself.
I stopped looking.
So, I don't know what is going on anymore
at times, I have the urge to take a look, but I don't.
Realizing I deserve better helps me stop missing
you. When I get the drive to look for you
I am able to control myself
the yearning of you is fading away
little by little and day by day.
It's scary, but it excites me
I feel peace
I feel at ease.
Wishing you the best from where I stand.
I hope one day you're able to stop fooling
yourself and seek for help.
You need healing no need to deny it.
Love yourself enough to know the only
person who deserves your love- is you.

-Jaymes B. Lazaro

I know what I can bring to the table
and I am afraid I won't be able
to find someone who can dine with me.

-Jaymes B. Lazaro

Your memory comes in waves
somedays your memory doesn't touch me
and other days it drowns me.
The only way I keep myself together
is reminding myself of the pain.
The words
the silence
the leaving me on read when I poured
my heart and you said nothing.
Nothing
nothing
nothing.
As months pass by, I started to acknowledge
from the beginning, I was nothing.
Games, you sure know how to play those
you won
you took all that I have and destroyed me
completely.
I don't have the courage to let go of you
I'm fucking trying
nothing is working.
I feel dumb
I feel numb
I still fucking want you.
How pathetic does that sound?
Wanting someone who never once
cared a flying fuck about me.

-Jaymes B. Lazaro

I don't go to parties anymore
because I'm afraid of seeing you.
I can't see your face right now
because I know I'll break down.
I'm not trying to make a scene to
something that meant nothing.
Maybe next year
I'll be ready, but for now
keep them as your friends
I still got a lot to forget.

-Jaymes B. Lazaro

I still think of you
and that is pretty sad to admit.
Therapy helps for a while
then I lose the aid
and your memory comes again.
I can't help myself
I crave every inch of you.
I want to hear your laugh.
I want to feel you again.
I miss the taste of your lips.
Why did you do this to me?
why did I do this to myself?
A mystery I'll die trying to solve.

-Jaymes B. Lazaro

I've been fighting with myself lately
but I lose every time.
I want you and nobody else.
I'm seeing someone
it's hard living this lie.
Telling her how happy she makes me
but in reality, she doesn't come close to you.
My family thinks I'm happy again.
I guess the more I play along
the more I'll forget you.
And that is the thing
I don't want to forget you.
When I kiss her
it is your lips I imagine.
Every time she says my name
it is your voice which I reminisce.
When I feel myself inside her
it is you who I imagine being wet.
And when I cum it is your moaning
"fuck" that I think of.
I'm just with her because she helps to forget you
maybe I'm wrong for doing this.
But I don't think I'll ever let you go.
I'm just going to have to get used to
you be in my heart for the rest of my life.


-Jaymes B. Lazaro

I kiss her, and I don't feel a thing.
I kiss her, and your lips don't come to mind
anymore.
I'm with her, and I don't care what I'm doing.
I fuck her, and I don't get any pleasure out of it.
I'm losing the scent of you
that's a good thing, right?
I don't feel a thing for anyone.
I've settled,
not just to one woman to many.
Fuck you for making me love you
and fuck you for destroying the way I view love.
Fuck you.
I deserved better.

-Jaymes B. Lazaro

But one day I just stopped waiting.
I didn't want to hear "I miss you" or "I don't love
you, I never did" I gave up all hope of ever loving
you. I told you one day you will remember me
and I hope you fucking miss me. I hope you kiss
him and feel nothing. I hope you fuck him but only
get the pleasure out of it. I hope one day you feel
empty and I hope the memory of me destroys you.
I hope one day you think of me so much it kills you.
You destroyed an innocent hearth- a loving heart.
When the day comes, you will whisper my name
and wonder. Wonder the life you'd have if you
would've been straight with me. Once I would have
given my last breath to hear you say you love me
that was a long time ago, I've changed.

-Jaymes B. Lazaro

I am slowing letting you go.
I no longer fill with anger when I hear your name,
I no longer fantasize over kissing your neck,
I no longer lose my breathing when
I hear your favorite song.
Excuse me,
let me make myself clear.
I still crave your lips
but I no longer desire your presence.
I'm focusing the time I had on you back to me.
I am changing and not just physically
my mind is growing in ways I never
thought would be possible.
I tried for so long to learn to
hate you, but I can't.
Thank you for teaching me
this growing stage I'm currently on
I mostly owe it to you.
I will always love you, but it is time
to finally let you go.
I let you go.
Take care of yourself, princess.
Be happy.


-Jaymes B. Lazaro

*You help me understand her*


You only call me when you're lonely
and to be honest, I'm ok with that.
Nobody understands me
the way you sometimes do.
You listen to my problems
you advise this broken heart.
I think I'm understanding
where she came from.
You're helping me understand.
You share your hopes and dreams
you tell me how he did you wrong,
I ask if its ok to think of her when I'm
with you and you say as long as if it's ok
if you think of him when I'm inside you.
Nobody understands me the way you
sometimes do. Two broken hearts are
healing together and I'm starting to
realize you're the me I was to her.

-Jaymes B. Lazaro

Let her go it will be alright
she didn't love you, and she never did.
Stop thinking about her too much
now you know you meant nothing to her.
She was honest, so you can't blame her.
Cry all you need but you need to let her go.

-Jaymes B. Lazaro

In the eyes of the people
around us we are both to blame.
You gave false hope
and I was expecting too much.
They say we should just move
on and forget.
I'm sure they know both sides.
I tell them my story
and you say yours.
Why can't we just communicate
with each other?
Tell me, why can't we?
I would kill just to talk to you
and leave things on good terms.
Leave things in a way we both can
sleep at night and move on.

-Jaymes B. Lazaro

I'm going a bit crazy.
I see everyone around me
living happily
I'm not sure
if I'm worthy to feel at peace.
I've fucked up enough
I tell her I love her- truth is I don't.
I don't want her
I want you.
When I kiss her, it's your lips
I crave the most.
I don't know why I'm like this.
She tells me she loves me for who I am.
She makes me feel like I could be loved
But why couldn't you love me?
why can she
but you couldn't?
I'm falling apart,
not knowing what to do.
She wants marriage and honestly
I only want to marry you.
Lately, I've been fucking up
and thinking about you is not helping.
I've tried everything to keep you
out of my mind
but nothing is working.
I'm living a lie.
I tell her I love her but in reality
I'm still fucking in love with you.

-Jaymes B. Lazaro

She knows I write poetry
She often asks if I write anything about her.
I smile and change the subject
because all my words are only for you.

-Jaymes B. Lazaro

Even though you treated me like shit,
I still miss you. Your touch, your kisses,
the way you smiled at me. I miss wrapping my
arms around you. I just wanted to make
you happy. I wanted to protect you and take
care of you, but you wouldn't let me.
I miss the way you made me laugh
even though you made me cry as well.
My love for you is so strong that
I can't get rid of it even though
I want to forget you.
I just can't.


-Jaymes B. Lazaro

I'm walking away.
For me.
No more overthinking about you
no more comparing you to other women.
I'm ending it.
I'm tired of being tired.
I hate that I still love you.
I despise the man I was when I was with you
the attitude
the emotions
the aggressiveness
the jealousy
the lack of self-confidence
the man who used his heart before his knowledge
that man was the creation of all of your projections.
Yes, you fucked me up -you destroyed me.
For a long time, I couldn't even look at another
woman without getting the urge to destroy her.
I hate that man you created out of me
after all, I can't blame you for everything.
I'm sorry if I ever did or said anything that was
hurtful. Don't worry I don't hate you.
I'm doing great. I'm working on me.
Without you, I don't think I would've
ever moved from sitting on my ass.
No hard feelings, I wish you well
I'm happy to know I can still love after you.
Me I'm learning to love me.

-Jaymes B. Lazaro

I must learn to unlove you
how?
I have no fucking idea.
But I must start somewhere.
I need to start by not looking at your social media.
I need to stop romanticizing over your lips.
This is draining the life out of me.
I just want it to end.
I want this craving of you to
stop consuming my well-being.

-Jaymes B. Lazaro

I never had you.
And the day you told me you
never loved me and how tired
you were of this somehow you leaving
felt like I lost you.
You were never mine, to begin with.
But this pain in my chest says otherwise.
Why did you kiss me so passionately?
Why did you tell me you loved me?
Why did you keep coming back
when I had enough?
Why did you open the door
when your intention was never to let me in?
why me. So many men and you
had to choose to destroy me.
I will never understand your reason
and will never be able to forget.
You never wanted to be with me
but through it all, my mind made me
believe you wanted to love me too.

-Jaymes B. Lazaro

I chose me.
And you chose you.
At least now we know
we can never be.
Our egos are bigger
than our hearts.

-Jaymes B. Lazaro

It took me a long time to
forgive you and forget the pain.
I learned to live without you
that's the funny thing about this
pieces of you remain within me.
The way your hair shined
upon the awakening of the sun
the way you laughed at my puns
the way you kissed me
the way you told me you loved
me in my car at 2 am.
Pieces of you still linger from time to time.
I've put those memories in a safe place.
I deserve to be happy, even if that's not with you.
Just because at times I think about us,
it doesn't mean I miss you.
It merely means I haven't forgotten
the fierce woman I used to be in love with.


-Jaymes B. Lazaro

Some people don't let go of their broken hearts,
some people hold on to the memories that keep
destroying them, some people refuse to move on to
a new soul, some people don't allow the memories
to die in vain, some people never let the tears dry.
I don't know about you, but I'm that people.
I refuse to let you go and that is what's slowing
killing me and in some fucked up way I've learned
to enjoy it.


-Jaymes B. Lazaro

Holding on is draining me
I have to do my future
self a favor and let you go.


-Jaymes B. Lazaro

I need to heal and change for myself
or I'll destroy you, future lover.
Be patient.
I'm becoming the best version of myself
to be able to marry you one day.


-Jaymes B. Lazaro

Don't let a woman have to
tell you she doesn't love you twice
the first time she sounds cruel
the second time you look like a fool.

-Jaymes B. Lazaro

I thought I had lost this fight
naming you the women who broke me
months of pure agony, sad songs and bad days.
I finally came to realize that yes, it was you who
broke me but it was I who continued to replay all
the good and failed scenarios in my head daily.
killing me softly and if I didn't change my ways
I would've been scarred permanently.
I loved you, and a part of me still does
somedays I do think of your smile, your laugh
the way you kissed me. I can miss you but not want
you in my life again. Letting you go was not easy
every day was a battle. I had to control myself,
not check your social media, not romanticize about
kissing you or holding you in my arms.
The way I was able to let you go was that
if my brain was going to play the good memories,
I had to force myself and press play to the bad ones
too. I was holding on to nothing. I was putting too
much importance on the role I played in your life
than the actual truth. Only to realize, I was just
another man. You never loved me, and you never
did. I will never deny the feelings I once had for
you and maybe I still have them. But missing you is
much less painful than holding you in my arms
again, so that's how I'll leave it. Loving you from a
distance where you can't hurt me anymore.

-Jaymes B. Lazaro

"I never loved him, that's just who I am"
that's what friend1 told me you said
and then you tell friend2 you miss my friendship
but please tell me, what do you miss?
me or the way I loved you
my friendship or the way I kissed you?
I came back because I fucking missed you
only to hear more shit.
I realized there was no way in hell
I wanted a person like you in my life.
I may still struggle to let you go
but I'm finally coming to acceptance.
I could never love you the same again
and for that, it was pointless to
continue holding on to you.
Holding on to nothing.


-Jaymes B. Lazaro

Yeah, she fucked me up,
but at least I was the one who
had the balls to give love a try.

-Jaymes B. Lazaro

Instead of walking away
I should've told you I loved you
but I was silent.
I saw you break down in front of me
and I said nothing.
I'm sorry
I'm just not ready to love you
the way you want me to.
I still need a lot of healing to do.
It would be selfish of myself to keep holding
on to you when I know, I'm not ready.
Please hate me,
bash my memory
soon you will forget my name.

-Jaymes B. Lazaro

I used to believe I was not worthy of love
but then I kissed you and oh my,
I've never felt that before.
One day I will marry you
but for now.
I'll show you
every kiss
every action
every poem
every breath I take
it all belongs to you
my beautiful princess.


-Jaymes B. Lazaro

You'd be surprised if you meet
the man I am today.
I no longer yearn for your love
my eyes don't cry out your name.
I'm a different man now.
I'm not that boy whose heart
you played with.
I'm a better man,
a man whose heart you
no longer have access to.

-Jaymes B. Lazaro

It took me several sleepless nights and
several exhausting mornings to
drag me back to reality.
A reality that always exists without you
but I was too stupid to believe
you were ever apart of it.


-Jaymes B. Lazaro

I had to choose between
holding on to you
or
protect my mental health
and for the first time
I didn't pick you.

-Jaymes B. Lazaro

I feel stupid for reaching out asking
if we could try this again.
I did not cry like before.
I did not question my self-worth.
I did not have significant withdrawals.
I was not addicted to you as I thought I was
this time there was no emotion.
Oh my, how stupid do I feel
you're a cold-hearted woman whose
heart is not capable of feeling.

-Jaymes B. Lazaro

I will not stop
until I hate you
more than I
ever loved you.

-Jaymes B. Lazaro

For a couple of months, I turned my emotions off.
I made sure I did not get close to anyone.
I shut people out including those close to me.
I did not want to feel.
I wanted to forget
to forget to feel.
I cried every night
yet my heart never gave up on you.
I tried everything
nothing was working.
I still loved you
I still wanted you
I was breathing, but I was barely living.
Instead of hiding my true feeling
I decided to feel
to feel everything.
Shit, it fucking hurt
every day was constant.
Remembering the late nights outside your
house where we talked up to 4 am,
where I would rest my head on your chest
to hear your heartbeat,
when you would tell me "te quiero"
that one night you fell asleep in my arms.
Everything we ever did it was being remembered.
It was painful.
Craving you and not being able to have you.


-Jaymes B. Lazaro

I was tired of being in a
lousy relationship with myself;
for the first time
I started to fight for me.

-Jaymes B. Lazaro

You need to take a step
back and look at
how you treated me
and maybe
you'll understand why
I reacted the way I did.

- Jaymes B. Lazaro

In the end, it was I who lost his mind
and you who claimed to miss nothing.

-Jaymes B. Lazaro

Please get out of my head
I'm tired of holding on to
something that was never real.

-Jaymes B. Lazaro

I was the one who loved you
even when you pushed me away.
I was the one who cared
even when you showed me you didn't.
Falling in love with you was my mistake
a mistake that I've paid the full price of.

-Jaymes B. Lazaro

I am slowly letting go
and that alone scares me.
I've gone used to walking
around with the pain,
now that it is less painful it terrifies
me to think of the person I'll be without it.
I can feel it fading.
This time I will not fight myself
to keep you around.
It's time.
Time, I let you go.

-Jaymes B. Lazaro

There is no reason to look back anymore.
I can't fix anything by thinking
about what I could've said or done.
I have no power to change how it ended.
I need to
cut the attachment
go back to reality
and let it go.

-Jaymes B. Lazaro

Please don't confuse my actions

I begged you because I thought you were worth it,
not because I had no self-respect.

I missed/looked for you because I reminisce the
good times we had together, not because I thought I
couldn't live without you.

I apologized because I recognized that I had toxic
characteristics too, not because I want to shift all the
blame to me and make you feel like your actions
were justified.

Don't confuse my actions.
You don't know me anymore.
I'm not that naive boy.
I know where I stood.
I know who I was to you.


-Jaymes B. Lazaro

I never sought to be a man who was cheated on
especially by a woman who claimed to love me.
During her confession, there was regret in
her eyes and pain in her voice.
I've never seen a person so destroyed by their
actions. She kept asking what she could do to fix
things, is it sad to say I wasn't shocked by her
actions? is it fucked up to say I'm glad
she did it first...


-Jaymes B. Lazaro

It took me months,
countless tears,
therapy sessions,
sleepless nights,
to get over you.
But holy shit
I fucking did.


-Jaymes B. Lazaro

I beg you to please
let go of the sleepless nights,
let go of the messages that never came,
let go of the idea that things could go back
to normal because they will never be,
let go of the hand you once held so tightly,
let go of the kisses that now belong to someone
else, let go of the memories you keep holding on to,
please let go. It only gets better if you make the
decision do it. Stop making excuses
do you want to get better?
Prove it.


-Jaymes B. Lazaro

I don't know
what is sadder
the fact that
I still miss you
or
the fact that you
don't even miss me.

-Jaymes B. Lazaro

Even if it's a lie
for one night
can you please
whisper in my ear
"te quiero"
one more time.


-Jaymes B. Lazaro

She tortured
me with every
soft kiss.

-Jaymes B. Lazaro

Accepting the fact
that you never loved me
is harder than pretending
that I'm over you.


-Jaymes B. Lazaro

We were that secret that no
one will ever know,
the kiss that no one saw,
the memories that will never be told,
we were everything
everything yet nothing.

-Jaymes B. Lazaro

I can wish all I want
to take you out of my heart
but I know I'm not that lucky.

-Jaymes B. Lazaro

How do you let go of someone you never had?
How do you let go of the words said but never felt?
How do you let go of the kisses that were never
genuine?
How do I let go of the woman I made up in my
head?

"You go back to reality; you can't hold on
to something that was never real"


-Jaymes B. Lazaro

When I meet you
I would've loved
to be the mature
confident person
that I am today
I'm pretty sure
I would've not even
looked at your direction.

-Jaymes B. Lazaro

I'll remember our late-night
adventures forever
but it is time I let go
and make new ones
on I go.


-Jaymes B. Lazaro

Use me
strip me naked
get on top and ride me
until you climax
undress my soul
and tell me you will
never let go
use me
tell me you love me
I've heard it all before
then leave, take what I gave
and never see me again.

-Jaymes B. Lazaro

Today I found your Ying & Yang
earing you lost in my car.
I drove all day holding on to it
that's probably the closest I've
been to you in months.
I rolled down my window and
tossed it out on the I-10
if you need it back, you should
find it on McRae exit.

-Jaymes B. Lazaro

*I don't want to love you anymore*

It took a couple of months
for me to break down
and let my heart know that finally,
it was tired of holding on.
I don't know where that last phone call
went from "call me in 15 minutes"
to a text that read "I never loved you"
The only way I live with this feeling
is to shout to the wind we weren't meant to be.
I'm tired of waking up feeling like I'm not enough.
I'm tired of pushing everyone so far.
Why did you tell you loved me?
And couple months later say I'm not what you want.
Tell me how did you change your mind just like
that? I guess your heart was never really in it
and now the only thing that's left is for
me to move on.

-Jaymes B. Lazaro

*This summer theme: heartbreak or healing*

Words said.
words torn
This year's humid hot hell summer
has a lot of things to be told;
no action
too funny to do
just words
the ones I remember
Oh, what will I do?
Keep the heartbreak or heal from it?
old battles never won
they say they never will
unless I decide
summer theme, healing

-Jaymes B. Lazaro

I ascribe the blame
to our, admittedly, unsensational sex
where the moans where loud
but our words were silent
where everything was felt
but nothing was touched.

-Jaymes B. Lazaro

She asked me to pick
between my past and her
and here I am still
writing about you.

-Jaymes B. Lazaro

She let me go
so easily,
that I started to
question every
"te quiero"

-Jaymes B. Lazaro

I don't talk about you anymore
because you still hurt me
in some hidden way.

-Jaymes B. Lazaro

I have a curse
of holding on to things.

-Jaymes B. Lazaro

I guess I am the
one to blame
I fell in love while you
just wanted to play.

-Jaymes B. Lazaro

I want to tell you something from the bottom of my heart.

For one second, I ask you to read this with the sound of my voice.

I forgive you. I forgive the pain. I forgive the lack of love. The lack of human emotion you gave. I forgive the man that you made me be. I was stupid for trying to make you feel something that you couldn't. I hope you still wear that gold choker because it looks beautiful on your neck. I hope you're happy. I hope you found the love of your life. I forgive you, even when you've never once apologized.

-Jaymes B. Lazaro

With the coldness of your heart,
your cruel words,
the toxicity of your actions,
slowly my heart started to neglect you.
It started to understand that it was never real
that I could not do anything
because you did not want to feel.

-Jaymes B. Lazaro

I thought behind your ego
there was a damaged woman
hiding from the world,
every time I tried to break your walls down
the more damage I did to myself.

-Jaymes B, Lazaro

I learned
to be ok
with your words.

-Jaymes B. Lazaro

I used to look
for you in every
woman I laid with.

-Jaymes B. Lazaro

Don't fall in love with me
I am not what you want
I tend to love truly
not cheat
I am real.
I'm sweet and romantic
don't fall in love with me
because I'm too emotional
and that alone will scare you.

-Jaymes B. Lazaro

I drank her silence like liquor
and it destroyed me the same
but I fell
for all of her
hopelessly and endlessly.

-Jaymes B. Lazaro

Self-control is power
don't text her
don't talk about her
isolate yourself from the thought of her.

-Jaymes B. Lazaro

The cruelest thing
she ever did to me
was make me believe
she cared.

-Jaymes B. Lazaro

I did not stop loving her
I simply adapted
to a life without her.

-Jaymes B. Lazaro

You left me believing
it was my fault you
couldn't love me.

-Jaymes B. Lazaro

And we just walked away
there were no more calls
the messages became less frequent
little by little there was no more us
I wonder, where did the memories go?

-Jaymes B. Lazaro

I don't write about you anymore
but today on my way home
"our song" started playing
it's been months since I last thought of you
is it safe to say my "Noches de Aventura"
were not meant to be lived with you?

-Jaymes B. Lazaro

I had a dream about
you last night
and I could swear
I woke up with the taste
of your lips.

-Jaymes B. Lazaro

I think it was the saddest farewell of my life.
Because after so many, this time I knew
she was going away forever.

-Jaymes B. Lazaro

I was supposed to see you again
we were supposed to talk again
we were supposed to fall in love again
but it was all in my head, right?

-Jaymes B. Lazaro

It wasn't supposed to end like this
if I could take back every word
I said that hurt you, I would.
I told you it was going to ruin
our friendship,
but you didn't listen.
I've been through this,
I already know how it feels to
fall in love
and not be loved back.
I know these next few months
will destroy you.
I've been there.
Today, I just happened to be
on the other side.

-Jaymes B. Lazaro

Call me stupid if you want
but I'm sure
I wasn't the only one
who felt things.

-Jaymes B. Lazaro

I hope you know
my words
still, belong to you.

-Jaymes B. Lazaro

I beg faith
to bring
us back together.

-Jaymes B. Lazaro

I am afraid once I get over you
I'll have nothing to write about
I think that is the reason why
I keep holding on to you.

-Jaymes B. Lazaro

I hope one of these days you may
stumble over my absence
and you decide to call me
when I'm no longer waiting for you.

-Jaymes B. Lazaro

Another night I've spent without you.
My heart asks why I keep missing you.
I'm dying to see you.
I have this urge to make love to you.
Another night without your love.
Another night filled with your memory.
The nights keep passing, and the more alone I feel.

-Jaymes B. Lazaro

I miss when you
used to want to give
us another chance.

-Jaymes B. Lazaro

I've always been the kind of man
that will always apologize before
I decide to let go
it's something about releasing
the tension between
my heart and brain that
brings me such peace.

-Jaymes B. Lazaro

I get asked a lot why I broke
things off with you that summer.
I was told I looked the happiest
I've ever been and I was,
very happy.
You helped me find my true self
you believed in me.
But I still believe it wasn't our time
you just got into medical school, and I knew
without me asking, you would've chosen
to stay for me.
I couldn't let you do that.
I had to make sure you left and fulfilled your dream
that's why I let you go.
I need you to live for you, not for me.

-Jaymes B. Lazaro

I like to think that at some point
along the way, we'll meet again
I get used to the idea that fate
has written me
in your future and my destiny
will take me to you.

-Jaymes B. Lazaro

*With Time part II*

I still love you, and that doesn't scare me.
I failed you.
I failed just like all the others.
You succeeded, you won.
You pushed me away, and I gave up.
I still remember that kiss,
the one that made me an addict for you.
I'm sorry. I know my insecurities, doubts, and
jealousy ruined any part I would've played in your
life. My neediness pushed you to your limits,
made you use words I to this day refuse to believe
you felt. I failed to solve the mystery of your heart.
I failed at loving you the way you needed to be
loved. It wasn't supposed to end like this. I hope
you don't hate me because I don't hate you.
There is no point in trying to take full responsibility
for something that I know I did not fuck up alone.
We are both good people.
Just not right for each other.
I will not be looking for you,
I will not text you,
I will not keep you alive in
my heart anymore.
I love you.
But your last text gave
me the message.

-Jaymes B. Lazaro

I tried to give it another chance
all she said was "do I have to block you this time?"
I can't say her reply broke me because it didn't.
I know her better than she knows herself.
I already knew that was going to be
her response, but I texted anyway.
There was a part of me that wanted to be wrong
there was hope that maybe if I did mean something
to her, she'd lose her pride and want to try it again.
I'm always right but this time I wanted to be wrong.
I wanted for her to prove to me that there was still
so much I didn't know about her, that I
don't know her as much as I say I do.
I was right.
I'm always right.

-Jaymes B. Lazaro

If they ask you about me, tell them

"He was the man I didn't love, and I was the woman who broke him"

-Jaymes B. Lazaro

*Una conversación con mi mamá*

"Déjala ir porque nunca fue tuya. Llora y grita su nombre. Pero mañana, te levantaras. Nadie se muere de amor. Abre los ojos. Desde el principio ella te lo dijo, que nunca te quiso. ¿Para que te aferras a una mujer que nunca te amo?"

- Pero mami, ella me dijo que me quería.

"Una cosa es decir y la otra es demostrar. Mijo por favor ya noté lastimes. Ya no la busques. Que ese mensaje sea el último que le mandes. Ya te dijo que si sigues buscándola te va a bloquear. ¿Para que buscas a una mujer que no quiere que tú la encuentres? "

- ya han pasado meses mami, y aún no la olvido. Me estoy desesperado. Ya no sé qué hacer para olvidarla

"Todo a su tiempo. Cuando encuentres una gran mujer, ahí es cuando sentirás lo que es el verdadero amor. Ten paciencia hijo mío. Pero por favor, ya no la busques. Para que buscarla si ya sabes lo que va a decir. Basta de humillarte. Basta ya. Amate hijo mío. Suelta la conexión que nunca existió. Hazlo por ti. Amate."

-Jaymes B. Lazaro

It's time I fucking listen to the
ignored calls/messages
to the "I never loved you" and
"do I have to block you this time?"
it's time I fucking listen to the woman
that you are not the one I want you to be.

-Jaymes B. Lazaro

Sometimes I wish you never let me
kissed you the first time I asked.
I wished we would've never
cross that line of friendship
because maybe today
you would still be a part of my life.

-Jaymes B. Lazaro

I want a 2 am phone call
when you're drunk
where it's your heart that calls me
I promise I'll pick up.


-Jaymes B. Lazaro

They say if I love her I have to let her go.
If it's meant to be, she knows where to find me.
Even though she was cruel when she left,
I still believe it is me who she will end up with.

-Jaymes B. Lazaro

Show me what it means to be yours
tell me what you do when you're in love.
Teach me the way of your heart
let me in, if we are going to do this again
show me, don't hold back.
Promise me you will show me love this time.

-Jaymes B. Lazaro

Remember last year we joked around,
and you told me to
ask you to be my girlfriend in September?
Well, its September now,
and what I'm asking is if we could
give us another chance?

-Jaymes B. Lazaro

I know you don't owe me love,
I know you don't owe me anything
but if there is any regret, any thought
of giving us another chance
look for me.
Tell me it wasn't all in my head
if you want to of course
or you can leave it how it is,
me believing you never loved me

-Jaymes B. Lazaro

People say with time it will stop to hurt.
But I don't want time to happen
because time means
seconds, hours and days away from you.
Time means you are moving on and forgetting me.
I know time will also help me forget you,
but I'm scared.
Because what if I never have enough
time to get over you?

-Jaymes B. Lazaro

This hurts like hell
I'm not a drinker
but I've been drinking myself
to sleep these days
I'm drinking because it's the
only way I stop thinking of you.

-Jaymes B. Lazaro

I refuse to accept you never loved me.
I won't listen to the words you used to remove me
from your life. I don't believe you when you said I
meant nothing. Every night we spent together you
can't expect me to believe you never once felt
something. You're not as cruel as you fake to be
every "te quiero" that came from your mouth
every kiss that your lips gave, every phone
conversation, every laughter you gave, every moan
you made, everything. I know you felt everything.
No, I didn't believe you when you said "I don't love
you, I never did" what I do believe is maybe you
got tired of fighting with yourself tired of giving
excuses to my actions. My jealousy, my neediness,
my lack of self-confidence. Tired of trying to
explain to yourself the life you would have with a
man like me. I can't write all the blame on me. We
are both equally at fault you got tired of my
emotions, and I got tired of the lack of yours.
Every time you left me hanging when I had a date
planned, every emotionless word you used to hurt
me, every unanswered text/ phone call, everything
we both did, we did it with the intention to hurt each
other. We both fucked up because the feeling was
there, the love was there we did not know how to
show it. After everything a portion of me still
believes in us a part of me still stupid enough to
think you cared about me.

-Jaymes B. Lazaro

Maybe I did love you a little insane.
I said things that you weren't ready to hear
I wanted to build a life while you
just wanted to see where this would take us.
I loved you crazy, and maybe that's why I lost you.

-Jaymes B. Lazaro

What do you say if I buy your favorite green apple Smirnoff and I pick you? Can we get drunk and talk about everything that went wrong? Because I still want to be close to you. In my head, I'm still all yours. I know I should give it up. I should move on with my life. I'd call, but I know what you will say. So, I don't. I'll intoxicate my blood with this 12-pack and hope I get you out of my heart. I know you don't care who I spend my time with. Lately, I've been doing wrong, trying to take the easy way out. But I can't. I still miss you. I still miss the poison of your lips. Getting drunk is the only way I go numb, and the missing you disappears for a little while.

-Jaymes B. Lazaro

How long am I going to have to
learn to be without you?
I don't think I'm strong enough
to watch you walk away
as if I meant nothing.
I don't believe you when you
said you never loved me.
How long do I have to wait for you to say
that you love me and that you're coming back?
Please don't make me wait too long.

-Jaymes B. Lazaro

Come back.
Come back and want me.
I'm not alright.
Tell me,
what have you been up to lately
I promise I'll listen this time.
Just come back
tell me you miss me
I've been falling apart without you.

-Jaymes B. Lazaro

Why does it feel so good?
Being together but we know we don't love each
other. You're telling me how he cheated
and I tell you how she fucked me up.
We try to forget what we can't,
and we silence our mind with a simple fuck.
You're moaning and screaming
rubbing your body against mine.
You're whispering sweet things
making me lose my mind.
Why do we do this?
Use each other to try and
forget the past.

-Jaymes B. Lazaro

How long do I have to pretend?
That it was all in my head
because I don't want to forget
what we were feeling.

-Jaymes B. Lazaro

*Can someone please tell me how?*

How do I remove her from my heart?
How do I stop thinking about her?
How do I move on when I still have some hope left?
How do I erase the taste of her lips?
How do I delete the image of her beautiful
naked body? How do I stop loving a woman who
made me feel as if I wasn't enough?
Is it a her problem or a me problem?
Who's at fault?
Someone, please send your
recipe of letting go,
I don't know where to begin.
Send help,
I'm in need of it.

-Jaymes B. Lazaro

I don't want love
if you don't come with it.

-Jaymes B. Lazaro

*Sunflowers were her favorite; I'm not sure*
*if they still are*

I have so many things I know about her
now that's she is out of my life
I don't know what to do with the
knowledge of her favorite things in this world.

-Jaymes B. Lazaro

I loved you more than you could ever imagine
I loved you with that colored hair that drove me
insane, with the passionate kisses, you gave,
with the soft "te quiero" you said.
I loved every inch of you, in and out.
I loved you like I never loved anyone before.
I loved you even when I knew you felt as if I wasn't
enough. I loved you more than I loved myself
that's where my problem was
where I depended on your love to fulfill
the emptiness in my soul.
I loved you,
up until I started to love me.

-Jaymes B. Lazaro

Somedays the pain is stronger
then my desire to keep
fighting for your love.

-Jaymes B. Lazaro

For the longest time, I tried to hate you. Only now
to realize that I can't. I wished I never kissed you.
That one minute of joy has turned into months of
pure agony. I wished I would've left it at hello.
There are so many things I blame myself for. Like
staying for the longest when you told me you never
loved me. I've made many mistakes and you're one
of them. I wished I could hate you but I can't.
Sometimes I think of you and all of the emotions
get the best out of me. I apologize for being a dick,
there was no excuse for that. I've learned a lot from
you and I thank you for that. I wish I could kiss you
one last time, hold you in my arms and hear you say
"te quiero" even if it's all a lie. Just one more time.
I need to let you go. I keep telling myself "today
will be the day" and every day just keeps getting
harder. A part of me still loves you. But I need to let
go. For me. To save me. Te sigo amando, pero adios
mi amor.

-Jaymes B. Lazaro

I fell in love with a cold-hearted woman
one of those who knows how to break you
and make you believe it's your
fault your pieces are falling.

-Jaymes B. Lazaro

I begged you, you piece of shit
do you understand that?
I don't beg anyone
and I only did it because
I thought you loved me
I thought you meant it when
you said "te quiero" but no right?
It was just my fucking imagination.

-Jaymes B. Lazaro

It was when you walked away
that's where I realized how strong I was.
Sleepless nights, hours of tears,
socializing but mentally not being there.
It was easy to lose myself with the absence of you
but I've learned from it.
It made me realize
it was a me problem when I depended
on your love to feel loved.
After you, I'd still have a lot of growing to do
I have to make sure I don't lose myself
with any other woman I fall for.
I'm strong, and I thank you for that.

-Jaymes B. Lazaro

I watched the
months pass by us
and there was nothing
that I could do I
just sat and watched
how quickly you moved on.


-Jaymes B. Lazaro

I pray to God every night
to help me find love
not with you
not with her
not with anyone
I ask him to send me the love
I've never given myself.

-Jaymes B. Lazaro

My first mistake was staying thinking
that every time you said
"why leave when you're so close"
just meant getting closer
to undressing you
not have your naked soul.

-Jaymes B. Lazaro

My past doesn't deserve
my attention and
that includes you.

-Jaymes B. Lazaro

Look at me
and tell me I wasn't
what you wanted.
Break my heart again
while you recklessly
choose the words
to destroy me.
Look at me
see the hurt splattered on my face
and then later hear you say
it was my fault for falling in love.

-Jaymes B. Lazaro

You should've seen my face when I read
"I don't love you, I never did"
and maybe then you would've realized
how in perfectly wrong I was in love with you.

-Jaymes B. Lazaro

I can't blame you for
destroying a piece of me.
You gave me a warning from
the start that I chose to ignore.

-Jaymes B. Lazaro

*I'm an addict for fictional love*

You were an illusion
who drain the life out of me.
Here I am, with my heart on the table.
Putting my ego to the side to tell
you I still love you.
And for what?
I did all of that for what?
So you can continue believing that
it was I who fucked this up?
When are you going to take accountability?
When will I hear you say "I'm sorry"
Or "I love you"
When will you fight for me the same
way I fought for you?

-Jaymes B. Lazaro

The moment I kissed you I felt something special, and I knew I loved you. If you can't feel it, I'll never be able to convince you.

-Jaymes B. Lazaro

*Fireball*

Lonely nights at the bar
I ask for rounds of two shots
one for you and one for me
I look around
trying to figure out if you'll ever come
back to me I keep drinking your favorite shot
hoping one day, you will walk in this bar
see me, and tell me you miss me
fireball gives me the warmth
I wished you gave me

-Jaymes B. Lazaro

My phone is quiet since you stop calling it.
I spend too much time thinking of you
chasing a dream I'll never be in.
The further you're getting the more it hurts.
I'm drinking myself to sleep hoping
this alcohol can help me feel you again.

- Jaymes B. Lazaro

I saw you
I saw you doing the thing
I never wanted to see
maybe he was just a friend
but you looked happy
I could hear your laugh
I felt your smile
I'm glad that you are happy.

-Jaymes B. Lazaro

I don't love her anymore,
but now and then when I see the color purple
I remember the touch of her skin.
I go to places where I wanted to take her.
And I don't love her.
I order a strawberry lemonade,
and I swear I don't love her.
I don't even know what's going
on in her life anymore.
Now and then she pops up in my head,
I wish things could've gone differently.
But we are two different people with
two different emotions. And it's ok,
I tell myself. It's ok if I loved more
than she ever did. It's ok. I respect it.
I swear I don't love her anymore.

-Jaymes B. Lazaro

I will always care for you
even after all the things you said
even after all the tears
I cried under your name.
No matter where I end up
I will always care
that's just who I am
call me stupid if you'd like
but I will never stop caring.

-Jaymes B. Lazaro

My journey with
love is not over
but it is with you.

-Jaymes B. Lazaro

I'm sorry
I still see her
when I kiss you.
It's not you.
Believe me.
I'm not your person.
I was feeling lonely.
I'm sorry I called.
I'm sorry I said I love you
when I don't mean it.
I'm too fucked up for this.

-Jaymes B. Lazaro

*9.17.2017*

You were my September love
do you remember
that one night
where my hands were sweaty,
and my feet were shaking
and I nervously asked, "can I kiss you?"
you looked me in the eyes and
said "why do you even ask"
I leaned close to you and kissed you
I was so nervous, but I played it cool
you were my September love I'm
still trying to delete.

-Jaymes B. Lazaro

We could've been lovers,
but we fucked it up too soon.

-Jaymes B. Lazaro

I wish I meant something to her
even if it was just a little.
Because if I did, maybe we
could've started it all over again.

-Jaymes B. Lazaro

Does it make me selfish
for putting myself first
or does it make you needy
for wanting my full attention.

-Jaymes B. Lazaro

But now
I don't care
not even that you
never loved me.

-Jaymes B. Lazaro

My love life in one word: interviewing

-Jaymes B. Lazaro

I'm still naïve to think
there is still time,
time for us to happen.

-Jaymes B. Lazaro

*Julieta (my car)*

You know who I am.
You follow where I go.
You hear me when I sing.
You're there when I cry.
You meet all the women
who come in my life.
You see all the rated R.
You see all the pain I hide.
I call you my pussy wagon
because you're my to go place to get it
and my go-to place to show my emotions.

-Jaymes B. Lazaro

*I am in trouble*

I lay with her
but I still think of you.

-Jaymes B. Lazaro

I wanted you
to be what I needed.

-Jaymes B. Lazaro

When she said she
wanted me in her life,
I believed her.
When she said
she missed me,
I believed her.
When she said,
"te quiero"
I believed her.
And when she said
she never loved me,
I had no choice but
to believe her.

-Jaymes B. Lazaro

It saddens me to admit
the first woman I fell in love
with did not love me back
it disappoints me to say I gave
all my appreciation to the wrong person.

-Jaymes B. Lazaro

I walked away
from someone
who showed me love,
someone who started to
help my mind forget you.
I left her because I was
not ready to throw
away the love I gave you
am I stupid or what?

-Jaymes B. Lazaro

I still see myself all over you.
I still see myself undressing you,
kissing your neck, sucking on your
breast. I still see you on top grinding
on me. Giving me a small
taste of the things that you can do.

-Jaymes B. Lazaro

"are you still in love with her?"

-I never stopped

Always

*The things they don't tell you about heartbreak*

Being surrounded by family and friends and still
feeling lonely. They don't tell you about the
sleepless nights. The feeling of being hopeless.
The physical pain you can't explain. The constant
scenarios of hope being played in your mind. The
draining. The weight loss. The drinking. The lonely
one-night fucks. The low self-esteem we are left
with. The way we view love in the end. The
damage. The tears, lots of them. The obsession
you developed trying to understand their reason
of leaving. They don't tell us about this, because
if they did. We would still look the other way and
risk it all.

-Jaymes B. Lazaro

I am sorry. Completely and terribly. I'm sorry for
falling in love with the way you said my name. I'm
sorry for loving the joy you brought to my life.
I'm sorry for every desire of your lips. I'm sorry for
being starstruck by your mind. I apologize for all
the times I told you I loved you. I know my
emotions were too much for you to handle. I'm
sorry. I know my love was too hard to be felt. I'm
sorry. Making you feel loved was a discomfort for
you. I'm sorry. I cared too much, and I know that
was something you weren't used to. I'm sorry. That
night when I cried in front of you telling you how
much I loved you-you weren't ready for that. I'm
sorry. I honestly thought you wanted my heart. I'm
sorry for assuming that you wanted it in the first
place. I apologize for falling in love with you. I am
making sense for all of this. It's still pretty fresh to
me. I'm sorry for feeling too much and
expecting the same emotion.

-Jaymes B. Lazaro

It started with one kiss.
It ended with cruel words
"I don't love you"
She followed "I never did"
She continued "I'm tired of repeating
myself to you, we are nothing"
Every word was painful.
But yet, I don't hate her.
I love her too much
that I understand.

-Jaymes B. Lazaro

I heard you're talking to your ex again.
Pretty sad if you ask me.
I know you love the attention he's giving you.
And for that reason, you still reply to him,
you notice him, and you are starting
to think of him.
The attention you give him
is the one I craved the most.
It's true when they say
humans enjoy hurt.
While you enjoy his return
I'm here enjoying your departure.

-Jaymes B. Lazaro

She only called me when she
wanted attention and since I have
no miss calls I know she has new company.

-Jaymes B. Lazaro

I think I miss you
Or maybe I can't get over
the way you made me feel- worthless.
And your return is the only way
for me to feel in value.

-Jaymes B. Lazaro

It's time for me to say goodbye.
It's his job now, to help you grow.
Make you happy, kiss you and tell
you that he loves you.
Accepting the truth is hard.
But it's time I stop fooling my own heart.

-Jaymes B. Lazaro

I hope this guy makes you fall
in deep in love with him.
Gives you flowers,
makes love to you like no other.
Treats you even better.
I hope he makes you feel all of the
emotions you claim you couldn't.
For you to realize, love does exist.

-Jaymes B. Lazaro

My heart doesn't feel a thing for you anymore. I wish I could make my brain understand that I don't need to keep checking up on you. I don't need to know how your life is. Or how that guy you're talking to is treating you like shit. Trust me, a part of me is enjoy your karma. But there is this other side of me where it feels sorry for you. This guy is your karma. I'm sure of it. I don't wish pain upon you. But if karma is doing her thing, that is out of my control. Good luck.

-Jaymes B. Lazaro

After all this time, I'm still struggling
to understand. Trying my best to
stay busy. I feel afraid ever to see
you again, I'm worried that I won't
ever be able to move on.

-Jaymes B. Lazaro

I know I'll be amazing without you.
If only I could just let you go.
My life can turn into something beautiful.
It's not healthy
isolating myself because I'm waiting
for the impossible to happen.
I don't know why I do this to myself.
It's over.
Stop it.
Fuck you.
Fucking bitch.
Wait.
Wait.
Wait.
Why couldn't you love me?

-Jaymes B. Lazaro

You were the one I couldn't get
and ironically the one I did not want.

-Jaymes B. Lazaro

If I could go back in time and
see all the arguments through your eyes
maybe it could help me understand
why you were so cruel.

-Jaymes B. Lazaro

I've been using you to fuck it all up.
In this empty mind, I blame you.
Where you took the joy when you left.

-Jaymes B. Lazaro

I'm a sucker.
I've been falling deeper
since that kiss.
When will it be over?
Why can't we be?
I don't need any
more arguments.
I can see how much
pain we give.
I need you.
I want you.
Be the one who I
give my heart to.
I surrender to your love.
I'm on my knees,
so please baby come back to me.

-Jaymes B. Lazaro

When she tells you
"I never loved you,
I never did"
Who gets the bad karma?
Me or her?
I wasn't perfect, but I'm pretty
sure I wasn't the one who broke
another heart.
So, who gets it?
Me or you?

-Jaymes B. Lazaro

And if you call me at 3 am,
but you're too shy to say anything.
I will listen to your silence.
Call me.
Even if you're still not ready to
surrender that you care.
I will listen
because I love you always
have and always will.

-Jaymes B. Lazaro

Big world
and somehow, I found you.
Don't make me wait too long.
Damm, you're gorgeous
these club lights don't do you justice.
Get closer.
Rub yourself on me.
You're turning me on
just by the way you're looking at me.

-Jaymes B. Lazaro

I was wondering if it
was a good time
to ask you out.
You know where I pay for
dinner and in return
you laugh at my cheesy jokes.
The perfect night
where I get to know you.
A first date is always a hit or a run.

-Jaymes B. Lazaro

It's only you and I in this room.
I never thought I would want to make
love to you right here right now.
Don't stop keep talking,
tell me what awakens your soul.
We should take this back to my place.
Don't stop keep it talking.
I'm so turned on.
I could fuck you here right now.

-Jaymes B. Lazaro

I joke and tell you I don't want you.
I tease you just a little.
I love that smirk you make when
you know I want to kiss you.
Roll your eyes at me again
and I'll show you exactly who you
want me to be tonight.
Let the music feel us.
Come here.
Get closer.
Spread your legs,
it's time I go on my knees
and hear you beg.

-Jaymes B. Lazaro

What's on your mind
Am I still on it?
It makes no sense to keep hiding.
Let's make it memorable
one last fuck
release my misery.
I need your body.
Don't fuck it up.
Tonight, it's just you and I.
Make me yours for the last time.

-Jaymes B. Lazaro

Do what you want to me
suck me
fuck me
ride me
I'm all yours tonight.
Tie me down
make me finish inside you
control my desire
tell me who is the boss of me.

-Jaymes B. Lazaro

I'm a sinner.
But with you, it's worth it.
I've made a name for myself.
Without you, I don't want to hear it.
They say I'm a player
but I'm only in the game for you.
You know I love being a sinner
but only with you.

-Jaymes B. Lazaro

Where is the love?
I'm kidding
I don't care
continue undressing me
make me cum
and if I moan "I love you"
it's not you who I love
it's that tight flesh of yours that I adore.

-Jaymes B. Lazaro

I keep using her body to try
and forget yours.
I know it's a dick move,
but it's the only thing that
I know how to do.

-Jaymes B. Lazaro

Quiet exit
is my way to go
my feet don't make a sound
as I tremble out the door.

-Jaymes B. Lazaro

She tells me I'm damaged goods.
She asks why did I decide to feel nothing.
I don't know. I wished I did.
All I seek is friendship.
Nothing more. Nothing less.

-Jaymes B. Lazaro

I saw her, and I knew
she had to be mine.
Not for life
just for tonight.
Her body made me tremble.
I needed to feel myself inside her.
I told the universe I needed her more
than I needed air.
I kissed her, and there I found the
universe had answered me.
With one kiss, she took my breath away.
She was a biter,
the best I ever had.

-Jaymes B. Lazaro

Summer is gone
time is passing.
I'm running out of excuses
to not love again.


-Jaymes B. Lazaro

How do I tell you I think about you every day?
How do I tell you I've never laughed with
anyone the way I do with you?
That I want no one but you?
How can I continue to love you
when I'm not what you want?
How do I stop missing you?
How do I stop thinking about you?
How do I tell you I love you without
feeling like I'm bothering you?
How?

-Jaymes B. Lazaro

You were everything
that I wanted.
I couldn't resist.
I wrapped myself in
your mind games
hoping one day you'd
stop playing.


-Jaymes B. Lazaro

I didn't know I struggled
with low self-esteem
until I met her.
I begged.
I cried.
Fell in her trap again and again.
She loved me
then she didn't anymore.
But I stayed
because I thought that's
what I deserved.

-Jaymes B. Lazaro

I'm too far gone.
You won't be able to
reach me this time.
Don't bother.
It doesn't scare me.
Now I don't even care that
you never loved me.

-Jaymes B. Lazaro

She dyed her hair blue
to match her mood
cold as ice
unforgettable like the sky.

-Jaymes B. Lazaro

The only thing she
opened up was her legs,
but I stayed because I hoped
one day she would open her heart.

-Jaymes B. Lazaro

It started as fun and games, where the kisses and the moans were temporary. Where her "te quieros" got lost in the wind. Sure I knew who I was to her, but my heart turned naive and started to make her to be a woman that she was not. I failed to solve the mystery of her heart, and she failed to try to puzzle mine. The flame was out way before it could be lit. The love was nonexistent to the ordinary human. She failed to see the extraordinary love that I was giving.

-Jaymes B. Lazaro

I'm sick and tired of letting you continue
making me feel as if I'm not enough.
I'm tired of you still being the one who
controls me even when you're so far.

-Jaymes B. Lazaro

*I've been having trouble sleeping*

You played me like a fool.
I'm searching for answers
trying to understand your actions.
If you didn't love me why fucking say it?
If you never cared why look for me when I left?
Those actions made me believe in us.
It might take me a little longer to move on.
But, when I do heal
I know forgiving myself will be the best part.

-Jaymes B. Lazaro

One day I'll listen to you say "I'm sorry"
then I'll say with a mouth that no longer
speaks of you "good luck"

-Jaymes B. Lazaro

Trust me when I said I loved you.
I loved you with all of your flaws.
With all of you berinches.
Trust me; I loved you more than
you will ever imagine.
You lied to me with every "te quiero"
Used words that will forever be
imprinted in my brain.
Destroyed my heart.
But I love you, I still fucking love you.

-Jaymes B. Lazaro

*Dear me*

She left
so, let her
keep walking.

-Jaymes B. Lazaro

Today I realized
that you not loving me
back was my biggest win.

-Jaymes B. Lazaro

My love for you is gone.
I have no idea when it all went away.
It feels like a new beginning.
Where the flowers blossom again
and the birds sing alongside me.
I can feel it
the air isn't as heavy
my love for you is gone
I'm excited to where this will take me.

-Jaymes B. Lazaro

It's over. With the deepest pain,
I have to tell myself; it's over.
I loved you until I could not anymore.
I wanted it beyond normal.
I wanted it to be you. To be us.
But I can't allow myself to continue believing
this feeling you claim I made all on my own
remain in my heart.
I forgive you, and I forgive
myself for loving you.

-Jaymes B. Lazaro

Maybe this was the way it was meant to be.
We were meant to cross path but not
stay on the same line.
I learned how to and how not to love.
How to forgive without an apology.
How to let go when holding on was still
what I wanted but not what I needed.

-Jaymes B. Lazaro

And if I ever see you again,
I hope my love for you projects in the air.
Where we can both feel its presence.
I'll smile from a distance,
and thank God for letting me see
you with my own eyes again.
Because that would mean,
God sent you to delight my heart
and for I to treasure
his decision as to why we
weren't meant to be.

-Jaymes B. Lazaro

I fell in love with you when
I wasn't trying to love anyone.

-Jaymes B. Lazaro

There is a fear in me
where I don't think
I'll ever get over you.

-Jaymes B. Lazaro

You weren't equipped
to be loved by me.

-Jaymes B. Lazaro

It's devastating the amount of hurt
we keep fighting to hold on,
just because we are not
ready to face the truth.

-Jaymes B. Lazaro

*I hate the things you do to try to get my attention*

Yes, I got the video.
Any other man would be at his knees
with that body that you were blessed with.
But not me,
I'm not like the rest of them.
All the fucks were fun,
But I've had enough.
I'm looking for more than elementary fucks.

-Jaymes B. Lazaro

I have yet to master the understanding of love.
I've broken hearts, and I've had my heart broken.
I've been a romantic, and I've been a dick. I've fucked,
and I've made love. Sometimes I wonder, will I die alone
without knowing the beauty of love? I'm worthy.
But will I be chosen?

-Jaymes B. Lazaro

4 am, and you're on my mind again.
If I could tell you how we can make this work
Will you listen?
Picture this, you and I again.
Let me tell you what we could be.
We can make this work.
Give me a chance to say I love you.
This time I promise it won't hurt.
Are you listening
or are my feelings still being ignored?

-Jaymes B. Lazaro

I need to be ok with being lonely,
I need to stop calling you when I miss her.
It feels good when I finish inside you,
but when I leave
she's still what I want.
She's still on my mind.
Midnight drives.
She comes to mind.
I look at the passenger seat of
my car and there she is.
Smiling and laughing listening to me
sing "wanted" to her,
I need to be ok with being lonely.
Because I still smell her perfume
when I'm with you.
I can't do this.
I'm too weak to try and forget her
when she's still all that I love.

-Jaymes B. Lazaro

You are the reason why I'm still holding on.
If only I could change the way my heart sees you
I know I'll be alright.
I keep telling myself I don't need you,
my life could be something else.
If only I find the courage to let you go
but my stupid heart keeps shouting that I need you.

-Jaymes B. Lazaro

I'm shouting your name all over Dyer
hoping you would hear me.
I swear If I make this right turn to
Alps Drive I could somehow
get you to love me.
But I go left.
Stop at the local gas station
buy alcohol
and drink my love for you out of me.

-Jaymes B. Lazaro

I keep yelling at God
asking why you couldn't
be right for me.

-Jaymes B. Lazaro

Loving her was not easy.
Because the more I loved her
the more I felt like I lost her.

-Jaymes B. Lazaro

*I promised myself I wouldn't bother you anymore.*
*Here is the message I did not send.*

I love you. I know. How can I say I love you after you've treated me like a piece of garbage, I don't know ok. I'm still completely in love with you. I miss you. I wish we could start it all over again. I wish I meant something to you. I miss holding you in my arms. I miss kissing you. I miss our conversations. I miss when you would talk to me about your problems asking for advice. I miss when you would share your good news. I want you. I miss you. I love you. I'm stupid I know. But I can't help but feel everything for you. Fuck. Búscame. Dime que no todo se fue a la basura. Dime que todas las veces que dijiste que no me amabas solo era enojo. Dime. Por favor dime que no todo era mentira. No quiero amar a otra persona. Pero tu silencio me dice que lo haga, que busque a alguien que me pueda amar. Si algún día me vez con otra, entiende que tomó todo de mi para poder olvidarte. Si me vez feliz alado de ella, admira la belleza que ella lleva dentro. A mi lado tendré una gran mujer. La mujer que me hizo creer en el amor otra vez. Y si algún día nos encontramos y los dos estamos solteros, tal vez en ese momento lo podríamos a ser todo correcto. Pero hoy, seguiré con mi vida y sé que tú seguirás con la tuya. Si el destino nos vuelve a poner en el mismo camino sabremos que tú eres mía tal como yo soy tuyo. Adiós amor. Te amo. Pero la vida sigue.

(Saved as draft message 08.09.2018)

265

I want to forget that night,
where "te quiero" came out of your mouth
because now I understand, it was just a lie.

-Jaymes B. Lazaro

I prayed to God for so long to send healing your way, not realizing I was broken too. And I am sorry. I didn't see what I had done. Who I was, and l am sorry. I'll continue praying for you. And I'll start praying for me too. And for us. If there's anything left of that.

-Jaymes B. Lazaro

Holding on to her was
like injection myself
with venom.

-Jaymes B. Lazaro

When I close my eyes, I can still see you.
The flower smell of your hair,
the soreness of my lips after every bite
the warmth of your skin,
the sound of your laugh.
Every chance I get,
I find myself closing my eyes to reality.
You may not be here anymore
but when I close my eyes, you still are.

-Jaymes B. Lazaro

You were the one
with the brutal words
and somehow I feel like
I'm the one that failed you.

-Jaymes B. Lazaro

You took my apology as if I'm taking
all the blame, making me the sick person.
It's ok though, keep pretending that I'm the
villain if that helps your brain feel no guilt
for the things you did to me.
Take my apology in whatever form
you need it to be.

-Jaymes B. Lazaro

I also had the opportunity to
treat you like shit, but I did love
you enough not to do it.

-Jaymes B. Lazaro

I ask myself if I was wrong
or right to love you but time
only reminds me that I was
wrong so fucking wrong.

-Jaymes B. Lazaro

*Karma said*

Let go; I'm in control
of her future now.

-Jaymes B. Lazaro

*To the man on Dyer*


You said things you shouldn't.
You used words not meant to be.
To a woman who was as scared as you were.
To a woman who never gave a shit about you.
You were talking nonsense when you
we're trying to make something out of nothing.
To that man on Dyer.
You loved but did not get loved back.
Stand tall and never return to that side of town.
Look around you,
there's a lot more than her.
To the man that no longer goes to Dyer
It's a memory you must put away.

-Jaymes B. Lazaro

*Therapy session*

Her love was not real. You made that in your head.
We talked about the things she said and the things
you did. You both were at fault. Take responsibility
for your mistakes. What you two had would've
never lasted. Stop replaying the memories. You're
delaying your process. Ok, you apologized, and she
said fuck off. Do it. Fuck off. Move forward. Look
at this picture. You turned on your car; your
destination is home. Now picture this. Every time
you're on your way home you to take the wrong exit
on purpose or you purposely drive on nails, and
now you have a flat tire. Both scenarios delaying
the time it would take you to arrive at your
destination. So here it goes. Every time you're
trying to move forward, you purposely keep her
alive. Stop fantasizing. Stop listening to the songs
you sang to her. Stop self-destructing. You can't
change the past so why keep going back to it? Love
yourself to call out your bullshit.

-Jaymes B. Lazaro

*Was this a message from God?*

You appeared to me in a dream
you begged me to let you go
and then you said
"here is the goodbye kiss you asked me for"

-Jaymes B. Lazaro

If I go, I'm going.
I won't come back.
Winter nights will be forgotten,
2 am conversation will be erased,
bites on my lips will heal,
purple will become my
least favorite color.
If I go, I'm going.
No worries.
I know you've been
fine without me.
I'm going.
I need to learn to be
fine without you.

-Jaymes B. Lazaro

my aim is to
move forward
is to not tell
you I love you.

-Jaymes B. Lazaro

And if everything goes well and
someday we see each other again,
what will I tell you?
How can I talk and joke with
someone who broke my heart so cruelly.

-Jaymes B. Lazaro

It hurts to be the person
who isn't chosen.
But then I tell myself that I
have not chosen someone too.

-Jaymes B. Lazaro

If you start missing me
remember I looked for you.
And you said
"do I have to block you this time"
If you find yourself wanting me,
just know you left me no choice
but to fight to move on.

-Jaymes B. Lazaro

We all have a choice
they chose to leave
without a care, if they left you broken.
Now, it's your choice to move on and heal.

-Jaymes B. Lazaro

*Alps drive is no longer on my map*

Sooner or later I was going to hear you're with
someone new. Who am I to blame you, you have
the right to do as you please. What I heard weren't
good things though. He treats you like you are
nothing. Only looks for you when he craves your
body. He doesn't tell you he loves you. He doesn't
make you feel like a priority. He and I are complete
opposites and somehow you fell in love with him.
I am not the one who was broken. I am not the one
who fucked up. I am not the one who wasn't
enough. It's you. I am a good man. Not perfect, but
good. You were everything to me, and you knew
that. And somehow your heart fell for someone who
treats you like shit. I was enough. Too much for
you. You're the one who doesn't deserve my love.
You're the one who wasn't right for me. You're the
one who's too fucked up to love. If he is what you
think you deserve, I'm glad you never cared about
me because I will never be him. I would never treat
a woman the way he is treating you. You fall in love
with men who make you feel like a dog. I'm grateful
you never loved me. Because that would mean I
was a man like him. And I am not. I'm better. I was
happy to hear the relationship you are in is not
working in your favor. Not because I wish you pain
but because I realized the only reason you didn't
love me was that I was more than enough for you.
You don't know how to love someone who loved
you. That's a you problem.

-Jaymes B. Lazaro

I wasn't holding on to you,
I was chaining myself to you.
Huge difference.
One is holding a love that
wanted to be loved.
The other is forcing love to someone
who doesn't want my love.
Chaining is not love.
And now it's time to break the chain.
I'm freeing myself from you.

-Jaymes B. Lazaro

Te jodiste porque la que perdió aquí fuiste tú.
Suerte con el pendejo que te trata como mierda.
Tal vez eso es lo que mereces. Pero yo por ti
ya no me preocupo.

- Jaymes B. Lazaro

At this point I'm just happy
she is fucking somebody else's life.


-Jaymes B. Lazaro

Listen to what I have to say.
Comprehend the words that I'm writing.
I heard the new guy is hurting you.
He made you fall in love.
Now you're the one crying yourself to sleep.
You're going to feel what I felt.
Karma is at your door, it's time you greet it.

-Jaymes B. Lazaro

Dear heart,

I need you to listen to me. It's time to let go. She is
with someone new. And you need to accept that.
You need to stop waiting for the impossible to
happen. Live in reality. I'm not asking you to stop
loving her; I'm merely asking for you to let go. She
is out of your life. She is gone. Now please, start
living like it. Stop fucking around. That won't help
you heal. Make friends. Call that girl who saved her
number on your phone. Take her out. Live. It's time.
Time you start experiencing new things. Do it. Do it
for us.

-Jaymes B. Lazaro

I went back to her, time after time
because I lacked self-respect.
I let the people around us look
at me as the fool because of
my low self-esteem.
I fell in love with her because
I lacked self-love.
I'm here making peace with her.
She played me like a fool.
I'm learning to be who I am,
to love and accept myself.
I'm working on my physical
and mental health.
The woman who broke me is
also the woman who help built me.
I opened my eyes because of her.
I'm in the process of sculpting the best version
of myself, and in some way, I owe that to her.
She was my wake up call.

-Jaymes B. Lazaro

One day you will remember me. I promise you it will haunt you. Because then you will see that what you do to others, life does to you twice as hard. And when your heart develops a draining obsession trying to understand his actions, your heart feels heavy, and you feel worthless. Acknowledge that this is the pain that has your name written on it. Best regards.

-Jaymes B. Lazaro

This story is over.
I'm writing the ending to our story.
Whether you believed we had one or not.
This chapter of you is over.
The hope of us happening ever again is dead.
My love for you has come to an end.

-Jaymes B. Lazaro

*With time part III*

I'm moving on with my life now. This does not
mean I stopped loving you. It's about saying I still
love you, but you're no longer worth this pain. It's
not about hating on you or wishing you bad karma.
It's about finally having the strength to walk away
from you. All of you. It's about keeping you close to
my heart but far enough where you can't reach it.
It's about cutting this attachment. Moving on, to
new adventures. To new love. To a love that makes
me feel appreciated. To a love where I don't end up
hurting like this. It's about I finally stop looking for
you in every woman I meet. It's about knowing you
might be kissing other lips but having enough
maturity to wish you well. It's about love because I
love you enough to pray to God to put happiness in
your life even if that was not meant to be lived with
me.

-Jaymes B. Lazaro

She says she doesn't want love. Her heart is too weak to feel again. I tell her I feel the same. "Can you hold me tight when I cry?" She asked. "I'll do much more than that," I said. I kissed her. Tears were falling. Hers. I could taste the saltiness of her sadness. And the shivers of her love story gone wrong. She's unbuttoning my flannel shirt. Her touch arousing my skin. My body is asking for sex. But my heart desires her story. She pushed me on her bed, crawled herself on top. "I'm going to make love to you now, and when I finish I need you to leave" she said with authority. I nodded, I couldn't speak because her right hand was thrusting me. And her left hand was on my neck. All night she was in control. She came about 5 times and I not even once. My heart kept distracting me. "Are you close?" She asked. "Yeah" I lied. There I laid, admiring her physical appearance. Until she said " I need you to fuck me now" I stooped up, turned her around, her back facing me, I went in and out "Fuck me" she moaned. "Harder, faster" she shouted. Her body was tired, but I had just begun. "Get on your back" I said. She was biting, scratching, locking her legs around me. She came. I came. The night was hot. "Can you please sleep over" she kindly asked as she crawled herself like a baby in my arms. "I'll do much more than that" I said while I gently kissed her forehead. "I can feel you're going to be right for me, as I am going to remind you the beauty of life" she said as she struggle to keep her eyes open. Her head was on my chest. For the first time in months, I did not cry myself to sleep.
 -Jaymes B. Lazaro

*The night she cooked dinner*

I walked in, and I could feel she was going to make a move. One look around and I could sense the sexual tension. She looked gorgeous. She was wearing a red tight fitted dress - her lips wearing a nude color. We finished a bottle of wine. She took me to her room to show me her collection of books. There was passion in her eyes. And her smile made me believe again. We went from her books to her shoe collection. From small talk to having sex. When it was all done she said "I think I'm falling in love with you" she tried to kiss me, but I backed away. I wanted to say it back, but I was so fucking afraid. I haven't seen her ever since because I am scared to fall in love again.

-Jaymes B. Lazaro

*The rose collection*

I had everything planned. The sunflowers, red roses, mint vanilla candles, I had just picked up your favorite chicken alfredo, blankets, my telescope was in my trunk. The night sky was beautiful waiting to be viewed by us. I had a ring in my pocket. It matched with that gold choker. The ring was a symbol; I wanted to let you know for the first time in my life, you were the one who had woken my heart. The ring was not to pressure you to start a relationship it was just a simple gift. I called. You didn't answer. The food was getting cold, and my heart began to wonder. Then you texted and cancelled. I would be lying if I told you it didn't hurt. My efforts were just not enough for you. Well, the ones you saw because there were many romantic gestures I planned and you never got the chance to see. I blamed myself for every failed scenario. You made me feel worthless. Like I wasn't enough for you. With time passing, I've lost that touched of me - that kind caring man that I was. I've meet beautiful women along the way who have tried to awaken him again. But I walk away because I am afraid one might succeed. I don't want it. The hurt. I rather die alone than cry myself to sleep again. She is not you, and I know that. I'm just too afraid to love again. You didn't just break my heart. Now, I'm a hopeless romantic who is afraid.

-Jaymes B. Lazaro

*It's like you meant something*

I spent months trying to walk away,
but you wouldn't let me go.
And I thought "wow she really wants me in her life"
I stayed after so many cruel words because
I honestly thought you were trying to open
your heart and let me in.
And then you let me go, like I was nothing,
like I was a bag of garbage.
And then I thought "wow this woman
never gave a fuck"
and I stayed trying to make sense of it,
trying to move on and trying to live
pass this pain. Then I did it.
Packed your memories, your lies,
your "I don't love you, I never did"
and your "te quiero"
I let them all go, not like you were nothing,
I let them go because you no longer
belong in my life.

-Jaymes B. Lazaro

Despite how it ended,
I know my love for you was real
you didn't know how to swim
in my waters to feel it.

-Jaymes B. Lazaro

Maybe one day I will find the right
words to say to you
even if you're nowhere near to hear them.
Maybe in a couple of years, we might
be good for one another.
Once you realize that I loved you
enough to change my bad habits.
I'm changing
I'm growing
I'm maturing.
I'm no longer that boy who said and
did all the wrongs things.
I'm different.
And that's another reason why I love you.
Because even if you broke me into a million
pieces with the words that you used,
I to this day thank you.
Without you, I would've never acknowledged
I have toxic characteristics.
I'm a better man.
And some part, I owe it to you.

-Jaymes B. Lazaro

She is somewhere out there
with somebody new, and it no longer
hurts to know that. I hope she is happy,
if not I hope she finds the courage to
walk away from anything that
takes away her peace of mind.

-Jaymes B. Lazaro

I won't beg anymore. You made it clear you wanted nothing to do with me, so please don't hate me if you see me moving on. That was a decision you made for me. I looked for you that last time, but you just reminded me again how you never loved me. If there is any regret in your words. It's too late. I've learned to live a life without you in it. And if you're just laughing while reading this calling me crazy well I hope it's a good laugh. Because you won, you made this heart fall in love.

-Jaymes B. Lazaro

I hope that wherever you are you are well, I'm not a
bitter person; I hope you found the love of your life.
I don't think there will ever be a day where I don't
think about how you broke my heart. I'm doing
better though, I'm thinking about you less. I hope
one day you think about me. And think about from
all of the men in this world, I was the only one who
truly, deeply loved you. And you threw it all away.
I'm not resentful. I only want to let you know that
you will never find a quality man like me.

-Jaymes B. Lazaro

There are days where I think of you.
But it has changed. I don't cry myself to sleep
anymore. I don't sit with false hope. My happiness
no longer depends on you. But yes, I still might
think of you. But with every day you are looking
more like a memory, visiting just for a few second.

-Jaymes B. Lazaro

I will love again.
But until then
I'll keep growing,
I'll keep learning,
I'll keep working,
I'll become the best
version of myself.
I'll build a life I've
always dreamt of.
I'll be complete within me.
So, one day
When love comes
knocking at my door
I'll be ready.

-Jaymes B. Lazaro

In this hot summer city, I drink myself to sleep.
Still not feeling warm enough I pile
blankets on my cold heart.
At night, my sweat fills my body.
It feels like a detox from you.
This is my body showing
I am letting you go.
My soul is cleansing.
I woke up to you no longer
having a place in my heart.

-Jayme B. Lazaro

At some point, you will realize the next step is
to walk away. Leave them alone. Someone that
is meant to be yours would be yours, and
who is not, no matter how hard you try,
will never be yours. Let go.

I woke up today with
a different view of
what we had.

-Jaymes B. Lazaro

I survived the worst depression of my life. Days feeling my heart broken asking God to help me understand what was happening. Wondering why you couldn't love me and why you hurt me without a care in the world. That's where I realized, and if I survived that, then I could survive anything. And if God already sent me the worst pain in my life, then I still have the best days ahead of me.

-Jaymes B. Lazaro

*Peace*

I'm trying to feel peace,
and I know how to get it.
I stopped checking up on you,
and I stopped asking your friends
how you're doing.
Every day you come to mind,
and every day I need to get you out.
It's a constant battle that I've been winning.


-Jaymes B. Lazaro

And the love I once had for
her became a memory.
A feeling stored deep in my heart,
locked away so it won't hurt any longer.
Her lips were no longer my deepest desire.

-Jaymes B. Lazaro

After you, I feared to look stupid again.
I promised myself never again will I
ever make a fool out of myself.
The truth is,
I haven't kept my promise.
I countlessly continue looking dumb.
The difference now is,
I'm making a fool out of myself but
with honest love.
The kind that feels right.
And even know some relationships
have failed but not one has made me feel as if
my obliviousness was taken for granted.
I haven't lost my stupidity,
I just learned who to share it with.
Therefore, I know I will never look
like an idiot ever again.
Because there will never be
another you in my life.
Not again. Not never.

-Jaymes B. Lazaro

Remember love does not go to waste.
And remember if it did not
work out how you expected it.
Just know it was God,
he was protecting you.

-Jaymes B. Lazaro

Never become bitter because of them
continue giving your love.
But give it to the right ones.
I promise you when it's the right
kind of love, even if it ends.
The ending will not be a heartbreak.
It will be a healthy experience
you will cherish forever.

-Jaymes B. Lazaro

Love is not about possession.
It's about appreciation.
I thank you for showing me with my broken ego,
low self-esteem, neediness, jealousy and all
those things that made the weak man
that I was then, to realize I wasn't in a
place to love either. With you, I learned
what love is not. And what love can be
if I find it in me, first.


-Jaymes B. Lazaro

*And then you heal*

I just got home.
It's pouring outside.
I'm sitting in my car
watching each drop fall;
your memory hit me hard today.
The music playing is bringing you
back to my passenger seat.
I hear your laugh.
I see your smile.
I see you in the maroon sweater
you would always wear.
I see you playing with your hair.
I feel my lips kissing you.
I feel my hands all over you.
Just like the rain,
I watch my tears drop
This time they were tears of goodbye.
I've accepted fate.
I've accepted your cruel words.
I've accepted reality.

-Jaymes B. Lazaro

I believe the reason it took me this
long to let go was because of fear.
I did not want to give my heart
out to somebody else.
Write her poetry.
Buy her flowers.
Tell her I love her.
Fall completely in love with her.
And for her, in the end, to tell me I wasn't enough.
I feared to give my love and be left alone to feel it.
I was afraid. But not anymore.

-Jaymes B. Lazaro

It doesn't heal all at once, you know?
Day by day it stops hurting a little less.
The sadness starts to fade,
missing them is no longer.
And then one day you wake up,
and it is not them who you think
of first thing in the morning.
Time heals.
Be patient.
You will be ok.

-Jaymes B. Lazaro

It may well be,
you and I will never meet again.
Just let me say before my heart forgets you
everywhere I go your lesson will be with me.
I can say I've changed for the better.

-Jaymes B. Lazaro

The improvement stage begins within.
Don't hate them merely wish them well.
Forgive without needing an apology.
Understand without really understanding.
Make peace with reality.
And love
oh my,
love yourself enough to know
who deserves your love.
You.

-Jaymes B. Lazaro

Tue, Jan 9, 2018, 1:01 AM

"You're probably ignoring me but it's cool, I would ignore myself too I just wanted to apologize, you're the last person I would hurt and I am so sorry Jaime and please please don't bring yourself down, like there's 3,000,000,000,001 girls out there and one of them will make you happy. You deserve that and so much more ok. Don't hate me."

When I received this text from you, I could not understand it. I was too obsessed with having you that I was blinded to see reality. Now that I think about it, I wanted to force you to give me the love I desired. When all along I knew you would never give it to me. I wished you stopped looking for me after this text. Because I would've never fallen in deeper with you. Sometimes I wish this to be how it ended. But it's not. You were cruel. And I was too invested. You're the first woman I fell in love with, and you're the woman who broke my heart. But you're right; there are so many women out there that one will make me happy. You're right, I deserved love and so much more. You're right; I don't hate you. I don't regret falling in love with you. And I don't regret living months in excruciating pain trying to forget you. Now I understand what you were trying to say. You were never going to be right for me. It has taken me a long time to realize that. I struggled to say goodbye because I didn't know how. But I do now. Even when you've never once apologized, today I decided to forgive you. Because I deserve peace in my heart. I forgive you. And now I set this free. Sun, Oct 21, 2018, 11:13 PM

I had no confidence when I
was trying to love you.
I couldn't even love me when I
claimed to love you.
I had my own demons,
the ones that came out every time
you broke my heart with your words.
I used to hate the color purple because of
that weak man, it would provoke to come out.
When you threw me out like dead weight
and broke my heart for the last time.
I looked for help.
I couldn't face that alone.
Today, I'm different.
I'm loving another.
Me.

-Jaymes B. Lazaro

*Loving you was a beautiful tragedy*

They say we will always remember our first.
First crush, first kiss, first love, and first heartbreak.
Once we experience it, we never forget.
What I felt for you was extraordinary. I know it
sounds unhealthy, but what I felt for you, I've never
felt before. I fell in love with you, and I don't think I
showed it enough. Every time something went
wrong I used words I did not mean. I have no
excuses for the way I was. I'm sorry. I know you
better than you will ever know yourself. I know you
did not mean any of the cruel words you used. You
were angry. I get it. I fell in love with you
completely. It was the most majestic experience I've
ever lived. It was short, and it mostly brought me
pain, but I don't regret any of it.

-Jaymes B. Lazaro

*I'm ready to call you a lesson*

It was beautiful falling in love with you.
It was short and fast. Lovely and traumatic.
It was everything I would do all over again.
My feelings were genuine. Yours were never there.
You will always be the only one.
The one who destroyed me and ironically built me.

-Jaymes B. Lazaro

*One last time*

I gave myself a final night,
a night where there were no tears
only your memory.
I closed my eyes.
I kissed you, touched you,
heard your moaning "fuck"
Pulled your colored hair
and I felt you on top again.
I hear you say "te quiero"
I'm gifting myself this ending.
After tonight, there is no more you
I will hold on to.

-Jaymes B. Lazaro

And just like that, my heart finally let you go.
Wherever you are, whatever you are doing.
I wish you the best.

Do you remember that night I bought
hot chocolate and donuts,
and I took you to all the places I once called home.
Explained to you the growth I endure in each place.
It was a fantastic night up until you said
"Hey my ex lives on the other side"
There were so many red flags I ignored,
and that's why I stopped blaming you.
I knew all along the woman you were.
Letting you go has been the most painful
experience I've ever lived.
But I learned from it.
I'm careful who I spend my time with.
I don't ignore toxic traits.
I'm wiser.

-Jaymes B. Lazaro

I recall people would say
"time heals, be patient"
I never really understood
Because I wanted you and nobody else.
Times does help.
It helped this broken heart heal.
I don't miss you anymore.
I'm not in love with you either.
But I still care.
I hope you find peace, love, and success.
We had a great friendship,
if you ever need anything,
I'm one phone call away.

-Jaymes B. Lazaro

Letting go is a process. One day you wake up, and they are still everything you want. Other days you wake up, and you hate them with a passion. And in between these moments, we end up finding ourselves. We may not see it because all of our focus is still on them but once you find the courage to fight for your peace, you will. Baby steps. It's ok if it takes you days, months or even a year. Letting go requires your full attention. I know it's hard. Your life still surrounds them. Keep fighting. Feel everything. Trust the process. One day it will be less painful, and their memory won't control your mind anymore. Let go when you're ready to let go. You're probably asking yourself right now "But when, when will I know I'm letting go?" The answer lays in the question. It's not in the " how do I know" It's in the "letting go" you'll know when you're healing. It doesn't happen overnight. You will sleep on it until one day your heart doesn't even remember to remember the love you kept holding on. One day you will wake up, and the air will be less heavy I will tell you one thing; you will never stop loving them. So please stop trying to. Healing is forgiving not forgetting.

-Jaymes B. Lazaro

Do you remember?
When you said, I made it all in my head.
Listen to this,
I walked away many times.
And you kept looking for me.
Begging for my return, for another chance.
What happened to you?
Why do you think it was ok to say
I made it all in my head?
You know this,
I wanted to leave many times,
but you wouldn't let me.
But I was the dumb one who always came back.
I've written so much about you only giving my
writing a voice. At times I would feel guilty; my
point of view does not complete the story.
It's a blessing to admit I don't feel guilty anymore.
The anger, pain, confusion, and love.
I don't feel any of it.
I'm not in love with you anymore.
I used to be ashamed to say that out loud.
I thought it wouldn't give my writing credibility.
For claiming and crying over you and in the end
release that I'm no longer in love with you. I
thought it would give my words a takeout.
Having remorse was wrong.
This is the final stage of healing.

-Jaymes B. Lazaro

I wanted your heart to be for me
but your words were just lies.
You would kiss me so passionately.
You made me forget who I was.
Every time I told you I loved you, I meant it.
Months are passing, the more you keep
disappearing. The first thing that left was
the smell of your perfume and the comfort
I felt when I laid my head on your breast.
Then left your lips and the lies
that came out of them.
I remember when you would say
"can we try this again" and I like an
idiot fell in your trap again and again.
Your "te quiero" are disappearing.
With each day you feel less important.
I'm at peace with your departure.

-Jaymes B. Lazaro

*Te amé. Te lloré.  Te olvidé.*

Te lloraba. Te lloraba todas las noches. Empecé a tomar. Algo que nunca hacía. Cogía; a cualquier mujer que quería tratar de hacerme olvidarte, con mujeres que me amaban, incluso con mujeres que sólo buscaban sexo como yo. Me convertí en un hombre que no reconocía. Y todo por mi sufrimiento. Eras tú a quien yo culpaba. Han pasado tantos meses que mi corazón por fin te a dejado ir. Batallé, pero luché. De alguna manera te iba a olvidar. Fueran por las buenas o por las malas. Pero lo hice, con mucho esfuerzo y dignidad. Mi corazón ya no te pertenece.


-Jaymes B. Lazaro

I loved her
and now I don't anymore.
I sing that one song, and I'm happy again.
When I pass by my neighbor's sunflower garden,
I pray for her to have a good day.
I see women with colored hair, and it makes
me wonder what color she is wearing now.
I see her smile on strangers, and I get the
urge to spark a conversation.
I smell her perfume on another woman,
and I smile again.
And here I ask. God, we both know
she was cruel in the end,
but I ask you to bring peace into her life.
Bless her. Guide her.
Give her strength. And bring her love.
And if you ever get the chance, God, I ask
you to give me a sign that she is doing well.

-Jaymes B. Lazaro

*Pain*

I felt it.
I lived in it.
I owned it.
And now I set it free.

-Jaymes B. Lazaro

"I don't love you, I never did"

With these words,
you broke me,
but I survived.

-Jaymes B. Lazaro

This past year has brought a lot of pain. I developed a unhealthy obsession I mistook for love. I gave a lot of effort to someone who did not deserve it. I fucked around trying to become cold-hearted. I failed. I failed to walk away when all the signs were there. I humiliated myself by crawling back to her feet almost every time. I was naive to think words were stronger than actions. But I learned. And that is something I will never take for granted, a great experience.

-Jaymes B. Lazaro

I couldn't feel the goodbye because I refused to accept it. She was a chapter that had its ending written before its beginning. I was fighting to hold on to something that never existed. She was a lesson, not a curse.

-Jaymes B. Lazaro

I couldn't face you for the longest time.
I ran away.
I did not want to show how I honestly felt.
If only you could see me now.
Your weight has come off my back.
Your words have been erased.
Every trace of you has been terminated.
Moving on never looked so beautiful.
Your memory is not being remembered.

-Jaymes B. Lazaro

I remember the days where
you were everything to me.
Now, you're nothing.

-Jaymes B. Lazaro

*This is my goodbye*

I haven't seen your face in months. I've figured it all out. I'm not in love with you anymore. I don't worry about you. Not like before. I remember when I would ask God to give me all your pain; to send it to me as long as you were safe. I would ask him to take care of you. To send love your way. To protect you. To send you a sign that I was still in love with you. I remember asking him to do something in your daily life that would make you remember me. Last time I heard about you, you were with someone who was treating you like shit. I remember that night, when they told me, I went home and prayed. Not for you to come back to me. I asked God to send you strength. To help you walk away from that. You're beautiful in and out. I will never wish you pain. I wish you growth. You broke me. I'm pretty sure you know that. I don't blame you, now I understand why we couldn't be. One day I will love again. I don't ever think I will love her the same way I loved you, but I still have love to give, and that is something that excites me. Loving her will be different because I'm wiser. I know what I want and what I seek. And when the time is right and God sends me the right one, I will love and respect her. I will use the lesson that you gave me to be the best man that I can be. Now I know the purpose you played in my life. I will admit, it's been quite a while since I last asked God about you. Tonight, I will pray for you for the last time. This is my goodbye. This is the way it was meant to be.
-Jaymes B. Lazaro

*Time is the enemy I'm grateful for*

I saw time as the enemy
the more time passed
I could sense this feeling changing.
My heart is something else
since it let you walk out of it.
The world is beautiful again.
Winter is here, and it feels magical.
Saturdays are my date nights.
I'm meeting new people.
I'm enjoying the best years of my life.
My heart has changed since I let go.
And oh my, how wonderful does it feel.

-Jaymes B. Lazaro

I want to let you know that it wasn't easy, I realized that my love just wasn't enough. I ignored the emptiness in your eyes and all the times "our friends" would let me know you had told them you were talking to another, I ignored all the signs. I would never ask the questions because I knew your response would kill. Like did you actually love me or were you just bored? All the times you looked for me when I walked away was that love? What was it? Was that just to feed your ego? It doesn't matter anymore. It was a mistake. Because my intuition would always scream for me to run. Months have passed and I've grown. Time has passed and your memory has stayed behind. It wasn't as simple as it is today. Believe me. There were horrible days where your memory would haunt me. I knew one day you would walk away from my mind. I did not think it would feel like this. I made the decision to release myself from you. To open the door that you didn't know you had the key to. This might be strange, but because of you I learned to value myself and to love myself. Honestly, I want you to know that. I know life has taken you in another path, I hope you've changed. I hope you've found what you've been looking for. I loved you, and I don't regret it. Because I am human, I do have the power to love even when you were the wrong one to try and give it to. You were never right for me. Ya lo entendí.

-Jaymes B. Lazaro

*You never deserved me*

You'll fall in love with someone who doesn't love you as I did. And then he will break your heart. Then you'll know how it felt. You'll ask God for me to forgive you because then you will understand. You'll cry yourself to sleep. And maybe, just maybe. I'll come to mind. And when I do, I hope you realize that I was the best thing that could've ever happen to you. You lost a man who was madly in love with all of you. And you said I wasn't enough. This day will come. The memory of me will haunt you. You'll get the urge to look for me, but you won't. Because deep in your narcissist mind, you know I'm too good for you. And I deserve better.

-Jaymes B. Lazaro

Then I realized, that letting go
was the last act of love I did for you.

-Jaymes B. Lazaro

My heart let go.
My heart has moved on.
I'm breathing this winter air.
My body feels the cold breeze.
Last year in this season I was holding
you in my arms to keep us warm.
Today I wear the brown sweater of
mine that you tore by accident.
I'm wearing it not because it's a way to miss you.
It's a way that my brain finally understood that
you're the one who never deserved me.
I wear it with pride.

-Jaymes B. Lazaro

*Brand new man with a brand new view*

If I never lost myself when
I was trying to love her,
I don't think I would ever be
where I am today. I'm grateful.

-Jaymes B. Lazaro

The tears became frequent. The sleepless nights were daily. The heartache became a lifestyle. The obsession developed rapidly. The love turned to grieve. With time I was able to see her true colors. Purple looked good on her. She tasted so sweet and twisted her words to make me to stay. Manipulating me with her mind games. Controlling my actions with the miss use of "te quiero". Then she changed to blue. She became the cruelest woman I've ever meet. She knew she had me on my knees begging and all that came out of her mouth was "I never loved you". And for months on my knees I stayed, but with time the begging changed. I'm on my knees, but this time I'm thanking God for taking her out of my life. Thanking him for blessing me with the hardest lesson I had to learn. I don't know what color she is wearing now or who she is kissing. But all I know is that I painted her canvas. Created art. Set it free. And now I'm moving on to a new white canvas. Taking my time, because a masterpiece must be done with patience, love, and technique.

-Jaymes B. Lazaro

Break a writer's heart,
and he will write about you
give a writer love, and you will
become his reason for writing.

-Jaymes B. Lazaro

Just when I did not want
anything with anyone,
when I was starting to enjoy
my own company, you appeared
and made me enjoy yours.

-Jaymes B. Lazaro

*She was by far, my favorite kiss*


I told her she was just my type.
She laughed and offered to buy me a drink.
All night she was the one with the jokes.
She later offered to buy me the best tacos of my life.
I was hesitant at first because I don't like tacos.
I didn't tell her that. But I went with it.
In 10 minutes, I found myself telling
her my life story.
Her company made me feel at peace.
With guacamole on my lips, she was wild
enough to steal a kiss from me.
The way she carried herself aroused me.
Her intelligence infatuated me.
Never in my life have I ever met
a woman like her.
For the first time,
I could swear I made love
without touching.

-Jaymes B. Lazaro

In my defense
I'm not in the place to love
I'm not asking you to wait for me
I'm simply saying if we could take it slow.

-Jaymes B. Lazaro

I knew sooner or later
love would come knocking at my door.
I don't know what's right for me
I've been in pain for too long.
She says she will be patient and she
will be with me through it all.
I'm starting to feel.
I'm starting to fall.
I'm letting my guard disappear.
She holds me tightly
and kisses me so soft.
I look into her eyes, and it just feels right.

-Jaymes B. Lazaro

She has a heart of gold.
I swear.
Kind of like the one that I've been told I own.
Something about last night.
The moon gave me a different mood.
It started raining, and she said "come on let's go"
We were the two idiots dancing with no
music on an empty parking lot.
It was innocent.
It was pure.
There was peace.
Cars passing by but my shyness
did not show even once.
It was her and I.
I'm giving this another try.
Our hearts are gold.
But my heart is shining brighter
since the day I met her.


-Jaymes B. Lazaro

I watched her undress herself.
And the more clothing that dropped to the floor,
the less I noticed her naked body and the
more my heart realized it was beating for her.
I watched.
Until she gave me those eyes,
I picked her up, and I sat her on my lap.
I ran my hands down her spine,
sucked her breast, and then I kissed her.
There she said "make me yours tonight"
She started riding,
her moans got deeper and louder I had
no choice but to take it missionary.
I went deeper. Slower. Longer.
I was covered in her juices.
I felt her body shivering, her hands scratching
my back, her legs wrapped around me pulling
me deeper inside of her.
As she bit my ear, she moaned
"make love to me; I'm forever yours"
And like a soldier, I obeyed my orders.

-Jaymes B. Lazaro

I'm geeking
over you
and its
fucking cute

-Jaymes B. Lazaro

You're the kind
of intoxication
I'm willing to lose
my self-control over.

-Jaymes B. Lazaro

My soul found what
it was looking for
It founded it when
she walked in my life.

-Jaymes B. Lazaro

She tells me I have a kind soul
and all I know
is that my soul feels at
peace when I'm with her.

-Jaymes B. Lazaro

When I said
I only had pain to give
she showed me
I was lying

-Jaymes B. Lazaro

Since I've been with you
the entire universe is
shouting yes.

-Jaymes B. Lazaro

My blood feels
adventurous when
I kiss you.

-Jaymes B. Lazaro

She planted love in me
and now
I feel it growing.

-Jaymes B. Lazaro

Give me your hand.
Do me the honors.
Let's make love beneath the stars tonight.
When we are done,
rest your head on my chest to catch your breath.
Let me kiss your forehead,
tell you how beautiful you are to me,
show you how grateful I am
I promise you're getting the best version of me.
I am falling
more and more each day.
This time I am not afraid
because I know she's falling for me too.
Oh, how beautiful it is to love and to be loved.
She is everything I've been praying for.

-Jaymes B. Lazaro

She said

"I'm yours forever, rest your head on my breast, let me sing you to sleep"

"I love you" she harmonized

I want to hold you.
If we lose touch, it burdens my mood.
I can't go a day without loving you.
Day by day,
as long as I'm alive, my heart feels for you.
We will hold on to each other
until our days are over.
If I get lost, I know your voice
will bring me back to you.
Sing to me.
I'm all yours.


-Jaymes B. Lazaro

Running late on Monday morning.
Clock into work and I can't concentrate.
I got the memory of your touch.
I got the smell of your skin on mine.
I have the feeling of making you mine forever.
This might sound crazy,
a little too early.
But I think I'm falling in love.
I can't stop thinking.
Of the way, I made love to you last night.
I want to be with you for the rest of my life.

-Jaymes B. Lazaro

You can take a big army of wild men,
and I'd still fight every one of them
to be in the hands of this woman.
A woman like her only comes
once in a light-year.

-Jaymes B. Lazaro

*Hacemos el amor toda la noche*

Sus carisias son tan angelicales
sus besos me llevan al cielo
me hace el amor con tanta ternura
me muerde en todas partes
que placer hacer la mi mujer

-Jaymes B. Lazaro

Never did I imagine
she was going to be the dream
I never want to wake up.

-Jaymes B. Lazaro

I can't help it when you give me those eyes
I can feel you undressing me.
The way you look at me,
it's a weakness I've come to accept.
I hear you calling.
I can make you moan.
I can make you cum.
I can make you feel loved.
Oh, baby, you're everything I want to know.
You complete me.
Come here
get closer.
I know you like it when I take control.
Give me those eyes every day,
let's make love again and again.
Creating our own forever.

-Jaymes B. Lazaro

She dries my tears with her lips.
Guides my fears with her words.
Uses her actions to calm my anxiety.
She gives me love that warms my heart.
This woman is extraordinary; it's not luck.
This is God's word.
She is my happy eternity.

-Jaymes B. Lazaro

"Read me one of your poems" She seductively asked. I went on my knees, looked up, kept eye contact, and there I said "I'll just make you feel it" as I started kissing her bottom lips, creating the memory of the sweetest juice I've ever tasted.

-Jaymes B. Lazaro

I think I'm falling in love with you
so please baby,
if I'm the only one falling
let go of me before it's too late and
you become the name of my new heartbreak.

-Jaymes B. Lazaro

I'm doing it,
with fear left behind me.
If this works, I'll consider myself lucky,
and if it doesn't, I'll find myself blessed.

-Jaymes B. Lazaro

I am where I belong

To my readers,

Now, looking back as I write this I found myself understanding. I was a little obsessed. Too emotional. I was a dick. I insisted to be loved, yet I couldn't even love myself. I blamed others for my lack of happiness. I contradicted every stage. But I worked through it. I'm in a good place now. I'm happy. I found true love. I found courage I did not know I had. I'm at peace. If you found yourself in my words, good. Because soon you will be living in the best version of yourself. Trust the process. And work for the peace you deserve. Stop being the victim, give yourself value, and put yourself first. Love yourself, forgive yourself, and start living for yourself. True love is found within. Break the cycle. Take chances. Make yourself ready for something new. Be happy.


Yours,
Jaymes

A letter to the man that will marry her

Hi, you don't know me. But I once loved her too. She was everything to be. Maybe she will talk to you about me, or you've probably never heard of me. But I do want to tell you how I fell for her. This is my story. She was mean to the world. Like really mean. She had just got out of a relationship, and she was destroyed. We were friends, really good friends. She cried in my arms once because of him and as a friend I merely advise her that she will be ok. I saw her almost every day. Her sadness would kill me. I cared about her way before I fell in love with her. Like I said we were good friends. I never saw her more until one day she dyed her hair. Her mood change. It was like she was a different woman. She looked free. Adventurous. Happy. That's where the trouble began. I've come to understand that I was her rebound. She latched on to me because of how lonely she felt. Her break up was fresh and I wanted to save her. Only now to realize that I did not. Ironic, but she's the one who saved me. We talked every day. I swear she is marvelous. Her mind is like a puzzle. An addictive one. She is beautiful and not just physically. Her priority is herself and that is something I always admired from her. She has a voice. She's not afraid to speak her mind. She's sweet. She doesn't show that side to the world but since you are going to marry her I know you've fallen in love with her. All of her.

The good and the bad. I fell in love with her.
Completely. She once told me she never loved me
and holy fucking shit that hurt. I wasn't the man for
her. But you are. Treat her well. Make her smile.
Please take care of her -she is beautiful. She's
perfect. She is love. And just because she did not
show that with me, it does not mean she's not the
right one for you. Protect her. Let her grow. She's
everything. Love her unconditionally. She deserves
love. Love her until your last breath. She deserves
happiness. And that is you. Keep her safe. And if
you have a chance tell her I said "you will always
be my Cloe" it's nothing romantic I promise. But I
hope that makes her smile. Hold her and never let
her go. I wish you both happiness.

- Jaymes B. Lazaro
 a man who once loved your wife

For her,

You will always be the first woman who I fell in love with. Nothing that I do or say will change that. For months, I gave the world shit, I spent my time shouting at God, asking for an explanation as to why bring you into my life only for it to destroy me once he took you out of it. Just because I say I fell in love with you, it does not mean you fell in love with me. I wanted you to be what I needed, and I wanted to be what you desired. But in this world, we all have the right to choose who we fall in love with and who we don't and no one has the right to give us shit about it. I've come to understand that. Call me delusional, I don't care. But I fell in love with you in a way I've never loved before. Even if you deny it, I will tell you one thing. I did not make you kiss me. I did not make you tell me all of those sweet things. I did not make you tell me "te quiero". The small taste of your heart that you gave me, that was your choice. I did not make all of this in my head. I did not fell in love all on my own. I've come to accept that the love that grew in me, you gave that to me. I stopped playing the victim because deep down I always knew what we had was toxic. I know deep down you felt something for me.

If it all was a lie and it's true, you never gave a fuck about me. Let me say this, what a cruel human thing to do, I hope you find peace. I can't change the past or predict the future. But I can say the type of man I am today. I talk about you, and I don't recognize who is speaking, anger or love are no longer in the mix when I speak of you. It's more of gratitude and peace. The completion of this book has made me think about you a lot. It's a good thing. I've come to understand the role you played in my life. Gracias. Gracias por los besos, los recuerdos y las lágrimas. La última vez que supe de ti, me dijeron que te estaba yendo mal en el amor. Me parte el corazón al saber que sufres. Por favor amate. Tu sabes lo que mereces. Eres una gran mujer, el amor te llegará, ten paciencia. Borré tus fotos y tus mensajes. Pero nunca borraré la felicidad corta que me diste. Ya no pienso en como fallé o como tú me fallaste. Eso quedó en el pasado. Te deseo lo mejor, felicidad y paz. Ahora me despido. Adiós. Ahora el destino requiere que vivamos la vida loca. Se feliz. Cuídate.

With love,

Jaime

Thank you

16372829R00222

Printed in Great Britain
by Amazon